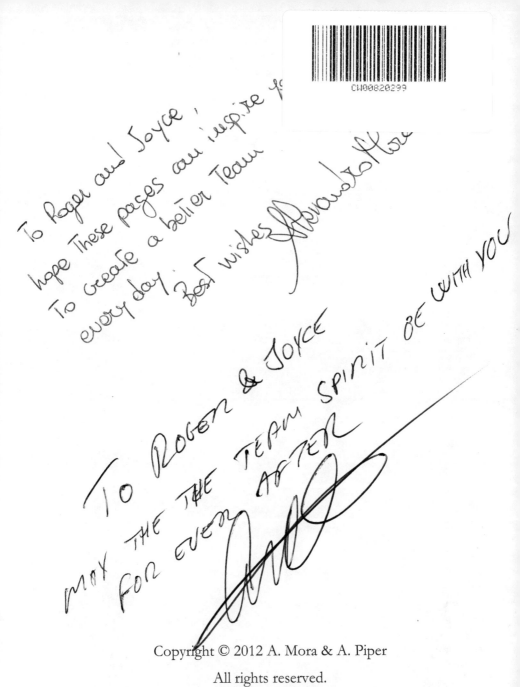

To Roger and Joyce,
hope these pages can inspire yo
To create a better Team
every day. Best wishes

To Roger & Joyce
may the the Team spirit be with you
for ever after

Copyright © 2012 A. Mora & A. Piper

All rights reserved.

ISBN-13: 978-1482549485

ISBN-10: 1482549484

CW00820299

Alessandro Mora & Anders Piper

DEDICATION

We dedicate this book to our Friends and Mentors Dr. Richard Bandler and John & Kathleen La Valle and we want to thank them for their continued support and inspiration. We would also like to dedicate this book to our families who have to put up with us, both when we are home and when we are away delivering trainings. Finally a big thank you to all the athletes, teams and coaches we have the privilege to work with. They are a true inspiration for what we do and our consistent drive to discover new ways of creating peak performance and making the impossible… possible.

ACKNOWLEDGMENTS

Reading the story you have come across some great tools and techniques. We want to thank Dr. Richard Bandler, Co-Founder of Neuro-Linguistic Programming (NLP), Joseph Luft and Harry Ingham for inventing the Johari Window model and finally Danish Centre for Conflict Resolution for their models on conflict management.

Cover illustration by SS Cheong.

Alessandro Mora & Anders Piper

IT ALL STARTED WHEN….

September 9

He was appalled and could hardly believe what he had just witnessed! John turned off the television and leaned back in his chair. It almost hurt to see a Football team with so many great players fail so miserably. No one seemed to be playing on the same team. Their starting players looked like they were lounging on a beach vacation rather than playing at the sports world's most elite level and the coach hadn't had the guts to substitute his failing stars with their new talent.

He went to the kitchen and looked in the fridge. He needed a beer, not so much for the alcohol buzz, but for the taste—and to get his mind on something else. It was strange that he still couldn't watch a game in any sport without getting so involved. Fifteen years as a top player and then a career of thirty years of coaching at the highest level of Basketball had left its marks on him. He would forever in his heart be Old Coach John. He grinned. "What a life," he thought as he opened a bottle of his favorite beer.

Coach John—John Craft— was a modest man in many ways. He had been a successful player when the money in sports was nowhere close to today's levels. Even as a coach, his interest had been more about working with the right team and the right organization. His successes in sports had granted him enough to live a relaxed retirement, but that wasn't what really mattered to him then or now. "What is money if the heart isn't in it?" had always been his motto, and he felt that now more than ever as he reflected on the game he had just seen.

He went to his back porch. He loved this spot where he could relax and watch the pond at the end of the garden and, beyond that, his neighbor's cornfields. He could sit here for hours thinking and enjoying the change of seasons and colors in the landscape.

His exit from pro sports had been planned for a long time, but he had kept it as a secret until the end of the season, right after his last trophy and then he announced his retirement. He didn't retire because he was worn out or because he didn't love the game anymore. On the contrary, he was perhaps more enthusiastic than ever before, but he simply wanted to do something other than hang around in sweaty locker rooms for the rest of his life. He knew he would miss it when he left, but he also knew there would be no better time to leave than when he was at the top.

As he had done after watching so many games before, he started thinking about what he would have done with a team like the one he'd just seen. He felt sorry for the team's young head coach. He'd never met him, but he had followed his career ever since he had come on the coaching scene. Vince Longman had a good heart and a good understanding of the game. He had taken many smaller teams to victory in the past, but this new organization seemed to intimidate him. Going from college to pro is a big jump. It's not the same—even though the pressure can be. This young man was probably one of the most promising head coaches in his sports and in the league. His skills in analyzing the game were stunning, but Coach John felt sorry for him. John could see that Longman was dealing with a group of players and an organization that surely were not in it for the love of the game.

Coach John thought about his early days in the pros. As a player and a team captain he had always focused on his heart and those of his teammates. When he transitioned into coaching as the youngest head coach in the league, that approach became his trademark and, ultimately, it built his legacy.

The phone rang inside. Coach John got out of his rocking chair and went to pick up the phone.

"John Craft?" the voice on the line asked.

"Speaking."

"I'm so glad I caught you."

Coach John was puzzled by the lack of introduction. The voice sounded like one in need, not a telephone sales person, so he allowed the conversation to go on.

"Are you alone?" the voice continued.

Coach John thought about being honest and saying no. His loyal dog was at his feet. But he thought better of the prank since this guy seemed to have some urgency in his voice.

"My apologies for not introducing myself," the man continued. "I had to make sure it was you and that we could talk in private before I went on. My name is Joe Ridgeback. I'm sure you know who I am even though we haven't met."

"The name does ring a bell," John said. This was a mild understatement. Most people in the country knew the name Joe Ridgeback. He was fifth generation in the Ridgeback dynasty and worth more than a small country's gross domestic product. Two years ago he had gone into sports, buying one of the biggest Football franchises available. He had invested heavily in the team, but didn't get the results he needed. The team's head coach wouldn't change his style, though. In return for having a bad season and still being inflexible, they sacked the old guy, bought new and better players, and then to everybody's surprise, hired Vince Longman.

"Oh . . . good." Ridgeback sounded surprised at not being clearly recognized, but he continued. "As you may know, I own a big sports franchise."

"Yes."

"Good . . . or rather I should say . . . not so good. We need help, Coach."

John was puzzled. "But why are you calling me? I never played or coached Football. Did you buy a Basketball team I am not aware of?" He didn't wait for an answer. "I know your franchise. I just watched that miserable affair minutes ago."

Coach John heard Joe Ridgeback sigh heavily. "That's exactly why I'm calling you. No one has a better understanding of players than you do. No one else knows how to generate a winning team like you do. I believe you're the one person in this world who can help us. I realize you played and coached a different sport, but I am not talking about game tactics here. We already have the best head coach in Football today and I'm committed to making him the greatest ever in the sport. He's young, but he has a unique understanding of the game. The problem with our franchise is not in the game plan."

"But what do you want from me—?"

"I want you to come work with Vince." Ridgeback sounded more urgent now and he spoke louder. "I want you to make Vince in Football what you are and always will be in Basketball." He paused and spoke more softly now, "I am willing to pay you very generously."

Coach John did not reply.

"Are you there?" Ridgeback asked.

"Yes, very sorry. I was just surprised." John was surprised by what Ridgeback said about him. Flattered, too, but he was also amazed by the man's guts and thinking. This young kid, at least compared to him, was willing to look at all alternatives in order to get results for his team. Coach John liked his attitude, but still wasn't quite sure what Ridgeback's expectations of him were.

When Joe asked him, Ridgeback replied, "Are you free tonight?"

"Yes."

"Good, I know you live out in the country so I can have my personal helicopter on your lawn in about an hour so we can discuss this one-on-one. Does that work for you?"

This guy sure doesn't waste time, Coach John thought. He smiled at the kid's sincerity.

An hour later he buckled into the passenger seat of a small helicopter. The pilot informed him that the flight would be about 45 minutes and that he should sit back and enjoy the ride. So he did and he started thinking about what he would meet when they landed.

*****

"I'm so glad I could talk you into coming. So sorry for the short notice." Joe Ridgeback looked like a Hollywood star. He had the build of a quarterback, solid, muscular and fit and his muscles were indeed well trained, judging from the firmness of his handshake.

"Well I—" Coach John was about to say that he hadn't committed to anything, but Ridgeback interrupted him.

"I know you haven't committed to anything yet. As far as I'm concerned, after this conversation, if you aren't interested, then this never happened. It's not my usual style to beg for help, Coach, but when I put my heart into something, I don't rest before it has been accomplished. I don't care about the money. I've got plenty. This is about the word that I've given to Vince Longman and the rest of my staff."

During his career, John had met a lot of young rich kids who invested in teams because they were bored and needed something to do. They wanted the prestige of saying they owned a franchise, but they couldn't care less about the coach, players, and staff. Ridgeback was clearly different. And John was beginning to like him.

As John expected, the Ridgeback house was enormous, but it was even grander than any other he'd seen. Ridgeback noticed him looking around. "I hope you don't think I brought you here to impress you," Joe said. "I am your humble host and I wanted to meet here so the press and paparazzi wouldn't be around trying to figure out what our meeting is all about. I wanted to make a personal connection with you, Coach, and a personal commitment to whatever is needed. I know you are a man of integrity and values and I have the deepest respect for you."

John almost blushed. Here was one of the richest people in the country offering him what sounded like the sincerest of compliments. "Thank you for the kind words. From what I hear, you are as well." But Coach John was not much for small talk. It was time to get to the point. "So! What is it exactly you would like me to do? You flew me out here in your private helicopter. You're obviously serious or I would be home eating a TV dinner on my front porch with my dog."

"A man who gets to the point! I like that, a lot actually," Joe replied. "Well, I'm sure you know about Vince Longman. He has what it takes to make this a championship franchise, but he's young. There are some things he doesn't know yet. Just because a person is good in one thing, that doesn't make them a champ at everything else. Vince could learn the hard and slow way—from making mistakes. But I believe in transferring competences. It's more efficient and effective to learn from the best, Coach. When we lost that game today, I saw what was going on. We need skills we do not have. I'm not just talking about the team. I'm talking about how we run our organization, the way we think."

He continued, "When I was a kid, my father, no matter how busy he was, would take time out to watch your games. I remember him saying over and over that I should watch you carefully because the way you influenced a team and an organization, that is the way to do it. You were my father's idol, Coach. I've tried for years to learn your techniques. I've read books about you in order to figure out what you did so well."

John wasn't sure what to say. "I'm flattered, Joe. But I just did what I had to do."

Joe nodded, "I know. That's what makes a good leader."

They laughed together, an icebreaker for John. Here at the dinner table was an old retired man and a young kid, but they had found a chemistry, one they would need if John accepted Ridgeback's challenge.

"How specifically do you imagine this happening?" John asked. "If I just walked in and took over, that would make Vince look bad."

"I want you to teach Vince. I have too much respect for you to tell you how to do it. I am convinced that you will see what needs to be done and you'll find a way to do it. You will do what you have to do."

John recognized his own words. "You sure know how to sweet talk a man." They laughed together again.

Joe leaned forward, "Now for the serious part! I don't expect you to be cheap, but I want you on this project. Name your price."

John thought, if he's asking me that question, he doesn't really know that much about me, but then Joe continued before he could answer, "I know you aren't motivated by money, but I want you to think carefully before you answer. The project is too important not to be reflected in your fee. I'll get you a brandy while you think."

Ridgeback exited the room, leaving John stunned. This kid is not to be underestimated. He's done his homework and knows what he needs to know.

The brandy tasted excellent, even though John wasn't much of a brandy man. Probably just some cheap stuff from the local supermarket, John thought, knowing better. He smiled and said, "I could get used to this stuff." They raised their glasses slightly to each other and after a moment Coach John continued, "If you don't mind me asking, Joe, what is this worth to you?"

Ridgeback thought a moment. "After my family and the name of my family, this is the most valuable thing I can think of. I want to show the world what can be done with the right people. To me this is more than just sport. It is life. It is the message to people out there that you can become anything. It is the message that you have to take chances. It is the message about the respect we should have for the concept of competence." He paused. "And for me personally, it is the message that even though I'm a rich kid, I take things seriously. And want to do them well."

John thought about Joe's answer while he sipped his brandy. What could he possibly ask for? He wanted his fee to be enough for Ridgeback to feel the pain, so that John would know the young man's commitment was real. At the same time, John knew enough about Joe and Vince and their team that he could already feel that the money wasn't the reason he would do this.

"Let me ask, Joe," John said, "why are you really doing this? Why take the chance on Longman? You could take a much easier route with the money you have, could get to the championship with a lot less hassle. So why bother? I hear what you say about competence and learning, but there are other good coaches out there, so why Vince?"

"I expected a question like that from you, Coach. Let me share a little secret with you that many people don't know. I trust you to keep it to yourself though." Ridgeback paused. When John nodded, Joe continued, "Vince Longman comes from a background you and I wouldn't even be able to imagine. Both parents were abusers and in early life all odds were against him. He grew up in a very bad neighborhood surrounded by criminals. At age fourteen, he was invited into the most prestigious gang on the block. They were dope dealers, car thieves, you name it. He was flattered to be invited in, but even more scared. He was naturally afraid of what would happen if he declined, but he didn't want to be a part of that world. That very night he made a decision. He decided that he would not waste his life, that he would not accept the cards life had dealt him, that he would become something and never look back. He packed his backpack, took 100 dollars from his father's wallet, left a note saying he would repay the money when he could. He took that hundred dollars and made it all the way across the country to his uncle. The uncle got Vince into a good school and, well, we all know the rest. His childhood isn't public knowledge because he wants it that way. He's never wanted special treatment because of it. I only found out, because I invested in a very thorough investigation into his background when I started putting my eyes on him."

John sat quiet in his chair, holding the brandy glass. He looked carefully at the curtains it left on the inside of the glass as he swirled it gently. Without looking up he said, "My price is one dollar." When Ridgeback didn't response, John sat forward and looked straight in the eyes of one of the wealthiest men in the country. "Whatever you would have paid me invest it in creating a talent school for young kids from the same kind of neighborhoods Vince Longman grew up in." Ridgeback continued to sit silent. "I know it's a drip in the ocean compared to the number of kids in that kind of situation, but like you said, we can send a message."

The two men stared at each other for a moment. Eventually, with a slow but firm voice, Joe Ridgeback said, "One year from now, the John Craft Junior High Sports Academy will open its doors and you can pick the hosting city." He extended his hand and they shook, looking at each other with a deep understanding about the significance of this agreement.

MEETING THE ORGANIZATION

"Would you excuse me a moment?" Joe interrupted the silence. "There's someone I would like you to meet." He left the room and when he returned, a young man in his early thirties followed him. John immediately recognized the young man, stood up, and extended his hand.

Joe began, "Vince, this is John Craft, better known as Coach John. John, this is Vince Longman."

Of course, the introductions weren't really necessary. From the handshake, it was apparent that there was a mutual respect between these two men, men with genuine hearts meeting each other in the right place and the right time, special people with the ability to make special things happen.

"I've been following you for a long time, Vince. You impress me!" John smiled at the young coach.

Vince blushed and returned the compliment, "I'm honored to meet you, Sir. I hope someday to have just a little bit of what you've got. You're my true inspiration."

"Well thank you for kind words, you are already a lot of what I was, I just have had more time to accumulate" John grinned. They both turned to Joe Ridgeback as if they knew what he planned to say.

"You both know my intentions. Vince, I believe you're the most talented head coach this organization has ever had. John, everyone knows you're the best head coach ever in any sport. With you two working together, we can build the most successful franchise in the sport. Vince as head coach and John, you are now his mentor, you will both know what has to be done. All I ask is that you both live up to your reputations of competence. Now, if you'll excuse me, I have a Junior High Sports Academy to start! John, I'll have a guest room made ready for you. We've got some clean clothes for tomorrow. I'm sure you won't mind if they're in our team colors." They all laughed. Then Joe left the two men on their own.

John and Vince got along right away and John could feel that he was dealing with a bright young man eager to learn. They talked—John asking questions and Vince answering as if in a job interview. Hours later, John finally slept in the guest house and Vince Longman drove home to get a good night's sleep before returning to the madhouse in the clubhouse.

September 10

The next morning, a knock woke John. The butler offered him fresh clothes, a toothbrush, clean towels, and a basket of toiletries. "Breakfast will be served in 30 minutes," he said.

In the bathroom, John smiled at himself in the mirror while he shaved. "What have you gotten yourself into this time, Coach?" he asked himself out loud. He laughed for talking to himself, but he knew he was already looking forward to the experience.

A letter from Joe Ridgeback was on the table next to his place setting.

Dear John,

I am very grateful for what you are doing and I am sure you are the man who can do this. I trust you and I want you to know that you can always reach me on the following phone number, 24 hours a day. Please keep the number to yourself as this is my private phone. If there is anything I can do to help, let me know.

Yours Sincerely,

Joe Ridgeback

*****

The limousine drove down the ramp under the giant stadium construction and into the VIP parking space right outside the elevator. The driver opened the door for John and the coach smiled at him. It was good to be back in the game, although this would be a very different one. A beautiful young woman greeted him from beside the elevator. Her slim figure was wrapped in a dress that probably cost enough for a family to live on for several months. She smiled and said, "Welcome, Mr. Craft. My name is Hollie. I'll be your personal assistant and help you around the organization."

John looked at her, young enough to be the daughter he never had but sexy enough to be a swimsuit model. He extended his hand. "Coach John," he said sternly. "If you ever call me Mr. Craft again, I'll fire you."

He paused then laughed. She laughed with him, but seemed nervous. Or perhaps irritated. John wasn't sure. Inside the elevator, he spoke in a friendlier tone, "I didn't intend to scare you. I'm just no good with formalities. If you and I have to work together, formal distance won't help us. John will do just as well, ok?" She nodded to John and gave him what seemed to be a genuine smile.

"I'll show you around, Mr. Cr—, John!" she corrected herself. "But first we have to get you an ID badge so you can move around freely. I suspect you don't want me trailing you all the time. Mr. Ridgeback informed me that I am at your full disposal. Anything you need any time of day, just call me." She paused. "Anything professional, that is."

She had set him straight right away, before he could even reply to 'anything at any time.' How she responded to what he could have said would have told him a lot about her. But she'd tackled him right off. He laughed so loud that he almost choked.

"Ha! I like that, Miss Hollie! It's for the best. With your figure and my age, you'd kill me anyway. I think you and I are going to get along just fine". He was still chuckling and she started laughing too. By the time they reached the executive floor they both had tears running down their faces.

The elevator doors opened and they stepped into the franchise's executive offices. John could clearly see this franchise was not short of money. His many years in sports had shown him successful organizations, rich organizations as well as many not so rich or successful. But he knew that money couldn't buy heart. As they walked along the corridor he looked carefully, noticing everything he could, listening, and trying to get a feel for the place. By the time they got to the last office, which belonged to the Head of Security, he already had a sense of something not quite right. He just wasn't sure what yet.

John was given his badge and electronic access to the whole building. The Head of Security had seemed uncomfortable at first. "I trust you're a very good friend of Mr. Ridgeback's," he said. "The team's General Manager Mr. Jives and me—we're the only ones who have this kinda access. Except Mr. Ridgeback, of course. In my twenty years here, he's never called me directly. I had to swear on my job that I'd tell no one about this. So my apologies if I seem a little suspicious."

John understood this man's responsibility. "Given your job, you have to monitor what goes on. I'm sure you're extremely careful to notice everything. It's only right that you act suspicious about this. Anything else would be negligence of your job. Everyone depends on you to keep the stadium safe for the players and for the fans. So I fully understand." John could tell by his reaction that the Head of Security was glad someone finally understood the significance of his job. He was still smiling when John and Hollie left his office.

"You handled that well," Hollie said. "Normally, he wouldn't be that cooperative. Of course, Mr. R did call him personally. I'm starting to like this assignment. Your next meeting is with Mr. Orlando Jives, our GM. I'll warn you up front. Only four people know the real purpose of your visit, me, Mr. R, Vince, and Mr. Jives. Mr. Jives didn't look so happy when he briefed me this morning and told me to call Mr. R for my instructions." She paused. "Just so you know," she added.

John had a feeling Hollie was going to be very good help to him. She came to a double door and knocked then opened it. They stepped into one of the biggest GM offices John had ever seen—in fact, the largest.

Mr. Jives sat across the room, behind an enormous polished oak desk. His back was to them and, as he talked on the phone, he was looking out the window. The view was amazing. John could see the training grounds next to the stadium and beyond those, the entire city after which the team was named.

"I don't know, he probably just wants more money to support his third wife or whatever." Mr. Jives shouted into the phone. He turned to greet his guests, looking stressed and out of shape. "Okay, keep me briefed." He hung up and stood. "Sorry about that. I had to deal with another one of those spoiled brats we call players. I'm Orlando Jives. Joe informed me about your assignment. No disrespect, but I'm not quite sure how you can help us, especially coming from a different sport, being retired, and so forth. But anything that can help is appreciated. Let me know what I can do for you and, please, call me Orlando."

John shook Orlando's hand. The GM didn't invite him to sit down. John tried to assess Orlando, but he was hard to read. Did he believe in this project or was he just pretending to because he was instructed by the owner? Time would show. He could sit down with Orlando later, but right now he was anxious to meet the players and the rest of the organization.

"If you want to see the circus in action, we have a press conference at 2 pm. Ought to be interesting!" Orlando said. "I'll be there. Vince'll be there, and our press officer Julian Swish. Of course, our beloved spoiled brats will be represented by Mr. Too Much Money and Mr. Vain, also known as Herb Withers and James Larson. They are our two so-called star players unless, of course, you saw them playing yesterday. Then you might call them our thieves, stealing our money without contributing. I just love my job, don't you? Oh no, you retired. Probably got tired of the same thing, right?"

John didn't know what to say. He had never been a fan of outspoken sarcasm and he especially didn't like talking about players as if they weren't human. Treat players—all people for that matter—the way you like to be treated yourself. That had always been his mantra. For sure there was a distance between Orlando Jives and the players— not that John couldn't understand his frustration with the team's performance yesterday. He already sensed that this was not only a problem with developing Vince's skills, but also one of developing the entire organization. Maybe he should have asked for more than one high school.

"I look forward to seeing the 'circus'. Like you said, it's been a few years since I retired but, you know, like the circus horse, hard to be away. In the meantime, I'd like to see more of the stadium and meet the coaching staff and players." He turned toward Hollie. "Perhaps Miss Hollie can show me around."

Orlando patted him on the back, "You've won the lottery today, John! Don't you be mistaken by her beautiful looks. She's got the brain of Einstein and the tongue of a politician and I don't know how many degrees from Harvard and Yale. Don't know what the hell she wants in this dump, but if brains and beauty can come in one package I am all for it. You're in good hands. No one in this organization doesn't like her." He grinned as they walked out of his office.

Once they were well outside the office, Hollie turned to John. "He doesn't mean to sound so harsh. He has a good heart, but he's stressed. He's not getting the results that the budget of this franchise needs. Coaches and players usually get sacked first, but he knows his job could be next. Mr. R is a very generous man, but he's also a businessman. Mr. Jives knows that, so he's frustrated by some of the players' attitudes. He feels like he can't really do anything about it in the middle of the season."

John nodded. He had seen it all before, but he still couldn't figure out what caused it all.

They took the elevator to the ground floor and rode a golf cart to the training grounds and the coaches' offices in the next building. They walked inside and knocked on the door to Vince Longman's office. "Hey Vince, you got a minute to introduce me to the rest of the coaching staff and the players?" John asked.

Vince took them to the large office the coaching staff shared. They were evaluating the morning practice session and still discussing what had gone wrong the day before. Vince cleared his throat. "Gentlemen, I'd like you to meet a very special person. I'm quite sure you've heard about the famous Coach John. I'm proud to have him standing here with me. Coach John, this is our illustrious coaching team."

John nodded and shook hands with each and every one, trying to assess how they responded by the look in their eyes and the pressure of their handshake.

After John had met everyone, Vince addressed them again. "You're probably wondering why a legend like Coach John is here. He's writing a book on great sports organizations and how to improve sports performance. He bumped into Mr. R who opened the doors to our organization. We'd like you all to cooperate with Coach John and answer any questions he has, even confidential matters. Coach John and Mr. R have made an agreement that nothing will be kept secret. When the book is published a year from now, the organization will be held anonymous. Any questions?"

All the coaches nodded towards Vince and John except one guy in the corner. John recognized him right away. Dumbbell Jack, Jack Keshigan, was this team's physical coach. He stood up, "John, you old bastard. Good to see you." Jack's voice didn't match the kindness of the words and John knew why. Early in their careers, Dumbbell Jack had been released from his job as fitness coach of the same team where John was a new assistant coach. John had convinced the head coach to implement a new way of physical training because it was easier on the players and didn't result in as many injuries, even though it took a bit longer for them to gain strength than Jack's traditional methods, and when Jack resisted, the head coach had released him from the program. "This is getting even more interesting", John thought.

"So how are you going to write about improving performance in our sport, John? What do you know that can contribute here? I mean no disrespect for the amazing things you have done in Basketball, but this is a different game!" Dumbbell Jack seemed pleased with his outburst and looked around the room for support. A couple of the other assistant coaches nodded.

John smiled and replied in a calm voice, "Well, Jack, you're absolutely right. I know nothing and that's why I'll have to ask you all a lot of questions. Some weirder than others, but definitely a lot of questions, so that I can find out what works and what doesn't. That's the purpose of my book."

Jack struggled to find something to say that could counter John's words but he gave up. "Well, like I said, good to see you again." This time there was a bit less resistance in his voice, but his eyes still gave him away. He was not pleased to see John.

"Let me introduce you to the players. They should be decent now, so Miss Hollie can come along if she wants." Vince walked them to the locker room and checked inside before he invited John and Hollie into the holy land of any sports team, the locker room. The smell of sweat and the damp air from the showers was unmistakably present as they walked in.

As Vince gathered the players, Hollie gracefully fended off thirty or so offers of marriage, which she was obviously accustomed to. Finally, Vince introduced John to the players much like he had done to the coaches. The players, less skeptical and more in awe at having the legend in their locker room, greeted John and welcomed him to their home of plenty, indicating that Hollie was a part of that. Their comments didn't seem to bother her and John thanked them for their welcome. He told them he looked forward to talking more with each and every one of them later in the week.

On the way out, John said to Hollie, "Tell me one thing. Doesn't it bother you that they talk to and about you in such ways? It seems everyone thinks it's okay."

Hollie didn't respond right away. When she did, her voice was not the young welcoming one that had greeted John when he arrived, but rather a sincere and adult voice, revealing herself in a way that surprised John. "When you're good looking, a lot of people evaluate you based on your looks and assume there is no brain. If you take the IQs of all of those players and add them up, they just might equal mine. But you know what? I really don't care. When I was invited to applie for the Personal Assistant job here, I knew I was fighting odds. Normally, in a sports organization like this, the PA is a male. But I like sports and someday I want to become GM in a big franchise. If you really want something, then it's all about making your mind up to pursue your goals. You may have a goal and you may be competent, but if you are not driven, if you are not compelled, then it won't matter. If you're driven and compelled, then no jerk who thinks that you're just a piece of meat can get in your way. If you allow other people's stupidity to stop you from reaching your goals, you are just as stupid as they are. I've decided not to be stupid! And not to be stopped!"

John was flabbergasted. He never would expect to hear a speech like that from this young woman. Boy, Orlando Jives was right. This woman is not to be messed with. He was pleased to have her with him on this project and wondered if the organization knew her real potential. He looked at her and laughed. "You're an amazing woman. Poor man who underestimates you! Where were you when I was still active? I would have hired you on the spot." They were both laughing as they took off in the golf cart to the clubhouse and the awaiting press conference.

*****

The room was full of journalists, including some that John recognized. Several recognized him too and looked puzzled by his presence. Vince Longman, Orlando Jives, the Press Officer Julian Swish, and Team Captain Herb Withers were on the podium. There was also a vacant chair for James Larson, the star offensive player. Even though it was 2 pm sharp, Larson was nowhere to be seen.

Julian Swish kicked off the press conference by welcoming the press and then passed the microphone to Vince Longman. He looked at the gathered journalists and started talking, slowly at first.

"Yesterday was a day that we will not repeat. We didn't play as a team. We didn't communicate as a team. We didn't perform as a team. Man-to-man we were a better team – are a better team. But we didn't utilize our potential." He picked up the pace, "and we did not play with respect for the many fans of this franchise from all across the country. We are not perfect, but even with a less than perfect execution, we should have played better. We have a big game coming up and we know we can do better if everyone performs to the level we expect. I know you like to discuss the past, but I would like to look forward to next week's game and focus on what we have to do. We need to tighten our defense, not allow so many mistakes, and keep up our offensive speed. That is our focus and our commitment this week. I believe some of you have questions, so fire away gentlemen!"

As the journalists bombarded the head coach with their questions, James Larson walked into the room and onto the podium in his usual casual style, as usual looking like a fashion model and in the latest fashion clothes. His personal sponsors included several of the most prestigious designer brands and he was very well aware of his marketing value to them. He had made it his trademark to show up late so that he could be more exposed and get the attention that potentially could increase the sum on the endorsement contracts.

After their many questions to Vince, the press turned their attention to Team Captain Herb Withers and wanted to know his assessment of yesterday's game. Herb stood up and walked to the microphone. "I think we did what we could yesterday against a better team on that day. We should have passed the ball more and played more aggressive with less focus on the defensive style that we have displayed in the first couple of games."

His words were so much in contrast to those of Vince Longman that the press smelled blood. They kept hitting Herb with questions, eventually focusing on next week's game. This time he looked towards Orlando Jives before answering. "I think we should go back to the style we used last season with Coach Mac. It's a better fit for the type of players we have, players like me and James Larson who can make the big games."

The journalists went wild and a desperate Julian Swish was barely able to regain control of the situation. He tried to do enough damage control not to be fired first thing the next morning. John stayed in the back of the room and was shocked at what he witnessed. Never before had he seen such an obvious back-stabbing from a player at an official post-game press conference. What shocked him the most was that, apart from a desperate Julian Swish, no one seemed to try to do anything about it. He wondered if Mr. R would appreciate this if he really knew what was going on. John thought about how he could change the behaviors in this organization. This was so much more than just building skills in a young head coach. This was war and he was mentally starting to get into his combat gear. This would be his ultimate game and he was in it to win it!

THE PURPOSE OF BEING A TEAM

September 11

Coach John spent the rest of the day talking to people in the administration and management. He had to develop a plan for where to start. At the end of the day, he checked into the hotel and arranged practicalities for his staying away from home. He had dinner at a nearby restaurant and ran into some of the players he had met earlier in the day. He had an interesting conversation with them and, away from team and the star players, they had acted with less intimidation and had helped John realize what was missing and where he should start. Before he went to sleep, John arranged a breakfast meeting at 7 am with Vince Longman, so they could start the work that needed to be done.

"You sure don't waste time," Vince said, yawning but smiling. "I really appreciate that you're doing this for me and the team. It means a lot to me."

"Well, we have a lot to do. I figured we could get to know each other better this morning and talk about where to start. Breakfast is the ideal time to talk about where to begin." John smiled at Vince and continued, "What is it that you want?"

Vince sat for a while, thinking before he answered. He took a sip of his coffee and said, "Well, the easy answer is a championship. The real answer isn't that simple. The truth is I want to be a coach and a leader who can guide my team to success, not just one season, but for the rest of my career. Success for me is not just winning the championship. That's important, but in my eyes, true champions act in a champion way. To me, building these men to become real champions, not only on the field but also outside, is equally important. When I coached minor teams, I managed to do that, but somehow I've not been able to get that grip here yet. Does that make sense to you?"

John was impressed. Vince had just described the perfect team with the perfect players and the legacy of really great coaches. He nodded and Vince continued, "When I imagine the future, I see the team winning on the field and I see the players going out and helping others win. I see them fighting for each other, backing each other up, and giving everything. I don't mind them making tons of money, but in my perspective they're losers if they have to brag about it."

John said, "What you just described is the end result, the thing you dream about, the place you want to be. My reason for starting here is quite simple. Just like a ship that sets sail and heads for the open seas, you need to be able to navigate. Knowing where you want to be in the future, how you want to feel is the first step. This establishes your North Star—the focal point in the sky that stays there even if you happen to get off course from time to time. I call that your desired state. Desired state is much more than just a goal or a vision, though.

The desired state is the mental state of mind you wish to have when you get there. It's living in a certain way, seeing, hearing, feeling things in a certain way and knowing from the start that that is the state of mind you want to be in and to have. It is knowing what the components of that state of mind are, so you will know when you get there. For me, the desired state includes the behaviors you want to have. The behaviors that can support the things you dream about. Let me give you an example. Let's say you dream about owning a red Ferrari. The question is, when you dream about that, do you dream about owning it or driving it? There is a big difference. In the first scenario, you have to focus on creating behaviors that will allow you to generate enough money to buy the car. In the second scenario, you have to focus on driving well enough to be invited to drive one or you could rent one to drive. Either way, you don't have to purchase the car, if driving it is your dream. So knowing the difference between the associated behaviors, we can then talk about what generates the desired behaviors. Behaviors are driven by the way we think. When we are thinking, we have both the conscious and the unconscious mind, and both influence your behavior and both can be influenced. When both conscious and unconscious mind are aligned toward a certain behavior, there is congruence in the mind and the spirit towards what you want and greater things can happen. Too many people focus on the end result forgetting about the behaviors that support getting there. To the fans and sponsors, the end result is, of course, important but for you as the coach it is about getting the behaviors that can get you there that you want. Once you have those behaviors, so much more becomes possible than just the end result you were initially thinking about. That's actually what I just heard you say as well!"

Vince nodded, but didn't say anything, so John continued, "Let's put this into perspective using European soccer as the example. You can dream about winning the Champions League, but to get there you have to become national champ first, and then play in the tournament, and qualify for the next round, and so on. The only question is this: Do you have what it takes? Of course, you need to have a great team of players. At that level, there's no doubt that we're talking about the very best teams in Europe, but they come from very different leagues with very different playing styles. Each league emphasizes different things. Nevertheless, they've all succeeded at the national level and all are the very best in their country. If the Champions League was only about the quality of the players, we could easily calculate who would win the trophy, but luckily for the sport and the millions of fans worldwide, such calculations doesn't always predict which team will win. In team sports, teams win because they have great players who play as a team. There's your dilemma! Your players don't play as a team right now. As far as I can see, the whole organization doesn't play as a team. Do you get my point?"

Again Vince nodded but remained silent, just taking in the lesson he was getting. John went on, "Once a player—in any level of his or her sport—reaches a certain level that separates them from the rest of the players, makes them stand out, very often they start getting different treatment from the coaching staff. Then they begin to expect different treatment. All of this feeds ego. Ego isn't a good or a bad thing. It's just the persona and, in sports, the ego often is an expression of the desire to win. It's stronger in the ones who want to get to the top. The desire is what makes them train harder, what makes them go that extra mile to win. As long as we are talking about individual sports, this can be a good, supporting attitude. But in team sports, it can lead to failure if not handled the right way. A professional soccer player once said that a top soccer team consists of 25 individuals, all focused on their own success, and the job of the coach is to channel all that energy in the same direction. That is exactly what we'll do here!"

Vince was taking notes now and replied, "I totally agree. It makes a lot of sense and, in a way, that's what I've been doing. But, like you said, the team and the organization here don't act as a team. I've not worked under those circumstances before. It's as if the money creates an environment where there are the star players and everyone else is their slaves, just working there to wipe their cute behinds."

John looked at Vince and replied "You know what? It's not just the money. I've coached teams with very little money that didn't act like a team. I've also worked with teams with lots of money and a mind-blowing team culture. So it's about what you do and how you do it. I want to ask you another question, Vince. Why are you a coach?"

"Because the team needs someone who can organize their direction and support so that they can develop both as individuals and as a team . . . and to win the championship!"

"Okay," John said. "Then what's the team's purpose?"

Vince looked confused about the question and responded uncertainly, "I guess to win championships?"

John shook his head. "When you have a group of individual talents, all skilled and all eager to perform and show what they can do, it is of outmost importance that their energy is channeled in the same direction. Many mistakenly believe that having a common goal such as a championship will do that for the team, but that's not the case. Every player needs to understand the purpose of being on the team. They need to understand what the whole idea of being a team is all about and how each player has to contribute to the greater unit called the team. It's the big 'why' question, so simple, yet for many so hard to define. So let's play with an example. Let's say that the team defines their purpose as winning championships. In sports, many would say that constitutes a pretty good purpose. But what happens if we challenge that? If the team's sole purpose is to win the championship, each and every player will focus only on that. That may, in fact, lead to a successful season with a nice trophy at the end, but how much will the star players support the new talent when the focus is only on this season? Then what happens if—or when—one or more of the stars gets injured? Is there anyone to step up? Many times not. Of course, with enough cash you can buy more talent, but those guys aren't going to just sit and wait forever. It's nice to be part of a winning organization, but for most players, it's even nicer to contribute. Rather be a lower ranked team and get to play than be benched or redshirted forever. Now, if we go back to the idea of having a purpose that generates more than just short-term results and we hold on to the idea of winning championships, we could add something about sustainability. So what if we say that the purpose of the team is to develop and nurture a championship organization that can go all the way?"

John looked straight into Vince's eyes and could see that this young man was getting it, so he continued. "Just by changing our words, something magic happens. We transition from end result to process. If we consider the team as an organization, things change. Every organization has various units, each with their own responsibilities and contributions, but in a successful organization, people work together. A team can thrive on a one-year success, but better to build a self-sustaining mechanism that can stay on top year after year. It's very much like a garden. If you only plan one year ahead, each year your garden won't look that pretty. Some plants just need more time to peak and show their real beauty. Holding on to the garden metaphor, you need to water the garden, weed out some things from time to time so other plants can grow. Occasionally, you redesign part or all of your garden to get a fresh start. Of course, sports is about trophies. Let's not kid ourselves! Nothing beats the feeling of winning. You never grow too old to enjoy it. It's that simple. But if you have a championship team that wins everything, there's always a risk for complacency. The attitude of 'we're going to win, no matter what' often leads good teams to lose. Competing at a high level in any sport requires star players, but once a star, how do you keep them there? How do you keep them motivated? A simple way is to make sure you always have new and upcoming stars knocking on the door. Thus we need to insert the idea of 'develop and nurture' into our purpose statement. This line of thinking requires guts in the coaching staff! What do you do when players don't want to focus on the team purpose? What if they don't care about the other players? Or don't want to mentor younger players?"

Vince was nodding slowly, taking in everything John was saying so he didn't stop. "If we look at a team as an organization, we know every organization has management and leaders, each responsible for developing and nurturing their particular department. They have job descriptions that state their responsibilities and against which they get measured. How many athletes have the responsibility of mentoring and nurturing young players outlined in their contact? We have the loose structure of team captains and that seems to work in some organizations. But why not make it the official duty of every star player that part of their responsibility and part of their bonus is attached to how well they perform that task? Great coaches develop and inspire leaders like that, both on the field and among the other coaching staff. On consistently successful teams, there's a spirit of passing on and mentoring, but unfortunately, we still see stars who act like irresponsible prima donnas, just taking care of themselves! So when you want to generate the team purpose of 'developing and nurturing', it's important that you think beyond the next championship and toward what you want in the future. Of course you can define a certain team as a project team with the sole purpose of winning the next tittle and there's nothing wrong with that. Just remember that this will also only produce short-term results. No matter whether the focus is short- or long-term, the purpose is all about why the team is there. The purpose statement describes in a short and simple sentence the process that you want everyone to focus on."

Vince looked at John. "You know what? What you're saying sounds exactly like the way I think. I just couldn't connect the dots. Now I do! We have to get the entire organization to have a joint purpose, to make this club one team. And it's got to start at the top so we can develop ambassadors in each and every department who follow the purpose. Not quite sure what it requires, but I'm certain that's what's needed!"

John nodded. "If you focus only on behavior, performance, and results, you'll only get short-term results. If you also focus on attitude, commitment, and feelings, you'll be far more successful in the long run. I've created a plan to help you and I made some calls last night to some friends and old colleagues of mine. Each one of them taught me a specific skill that I still carry today. Even though they're from different sports, I'm convinced you'll be able to transfer these skills to your team and make them a winning organization. I realize your primary responsibility is for the players and not so much for the rest of the organization, but if you want to be the coach you described a little while ago, you have to influence the whole organization. I'll help you, but you're the one who'll have to do it. Are you in on this one?"

John expected Vince's answer, but was still reassured when he saw the determination in Vince's nod. John extended his hand and the two men shook, creating a pact that would change this team.

******

Vince could hardly wait to get to work. As soon as he finished breakfast with Coach John he drove to the clubhouse and went straight to Orlando Jives's office. "Hey Orlando, you got a minute?" Vince asked as he walked into Jives's office.

Orlando looked up, "Always my friend. What can I do for you?"

"What's the purpose of our organization?" Vince asked.

Orlando laughed. "Well that should be pretty obvious. It's to make money for the owners. I thought you knew that!"

Vince thought about challenging Jives, but decided that, for now, he would just ask others around the organization to see what people answered. He thanked Orlando. As he turned to leave the office, Orlando waved him off as if he was crazy.

In the hallway, Vince ran into Julian Swish, the team's press officer. "Hey Julian, can I ask you something?"

"Sure. Fire away," Julian answered.

"What is the purpose of our organization?"

Julian thought for a moment. "It probably depends on who you ask. Some would say to win championships. I would say to make money. Why else would Mr. R invest all his money?"

"Thank you," Vince said and walked away. He headed over to the players' locker room. He met Dumbbell Jack in the doorway. "Good morning Jack, how's life?"

"Well, it would be better if these wimps could actually lift a weight without getting hurt all the time." Dumbbell Jack was grumpy as usual.

"Yeah, I know you've had problems since you started the new heavy lift program. Let me ask you something. It may sound a little crazy. What's the purpose of having a coaching team?"

Jack looked at Vince as if he'd just invited him on a trip to the moon. "You got to be kidding me with a question like that! Is that old Coach John getting you to run around asking stupid questions like that?"

"You really don't like Coach John do you?" Vince asked.

Jack just looked at Vince for a minute as if he was trying to figure out how much to say. "You wouldn't understand. I need to go to the weight room. See you later." As Jack walked away, he turned and smiled, "and the answer to your question ought to be very obvious to you. It's to win championships! It's really a simple world we live in." He laughed loudly as he walked down the corridor.

Vince stood for a while and thought about the look in Jack's eyes. At first he thought it was hatred, but now he had a different feeling. It was something else. He couldn't put his finger on it, but decided to ask Coach John to see what he had to say.

In the locker room, the team was getting ready for the morning practice. The assistant coaching staff usually led morning practice, so the players noticed when Vince came in the room. Many of them welcomed him with "Morning Coach!" Vince returned their greetings.

He picked up a chair and placed it in the middle of the room. "Huddle up, team!" he yelled.

The players surrounded Vince and he could see they were confused about why he was here. "Listen up guys! We've got an important game coming up next weekend. We, as a team, need to show the fans that we can work as a team. Many folks doubt this after our collapse two days ago. But I know what great players you guys are! I know if you put all that into a team effort, we can kick some ass!" He looked each player right in the eyes to get a personal commitment from each and every one. "I want you all to think about some simple questions this week: Why are we a team? What's the purpose of being a team? And what's the purpose of being this team?"

Notes to myself:

✓ *Know what you want, your desired state*

✓ *Know why you are a team, what is the purpose of being a team*

✓ *Think long term, plan for the future*

A SENSE OF DIRECTION

September 12,

Coach John and Miss Hollie watched the team train from the stands. Vince looked very confident and his enthusiasm was high. At the end of the practice session, they went down on the field to meet Vince. He ran toward them with excitement. He could tell by the way they were looking at him that something was about to happen.

"Good session today," John began.

"Yes, I think all the guys felt that something's changing," Vince said. "Everybody but Withers, I know he wants my head off."

"Don't worry about him yet. We have more important things to do."

"More important things than the star of my team who is trying to sabotage me? I'm sitting on a time bomb."

"I know, but I'm going to show you how to defuse that bomb and all the other bombs out there."

"Well! Now you have my attention!" Vince was clearly interested.

"Thanks to Miss Hollie, we have a very special appointment in 45 minutes."

Curious about the appointment, Vince took a quick shower and then joined John and Hollie at the bar in the clubhouse. They chatted for a few minutes before the mysterious guest appeared. He was tall, dressed in an expensive suit, and walked with confidence. Even though he was a large man, he moved with grace and his authority drew everyone's look. Vince recognized him and could hardly believe his eyes.

"Hey, Phil! How're you doing?" Coach John stood up and welcomed his guest.

"I'm great and you?" the man replied.

"I'm doing good. Still trying to inspire good thoughts in young people" John said and they laughed together.

Vince's heart beat like a drum. One of the best and most winning coaches in the world stood right in front of him. Vince had read all the books this man had written and every article about him. He had read or listened to every interview with him that he could find. Even though they had never met, this man was one of Vince's mentors.

"I'd like to introduce my friend Vince Longman" John began.

"Nice to meet you Vince, I'm Phil…"

Vince didn't let him finish. "I know who you are. I've read all about you, watched as many interviews as I could… actually you're my hero!"

"Oh well, thank you, son. I guess I don't need to introduce myself further then," and he laughed again.

Coach John was looking at the scene with satisfaction. He knew he'd gotten Vince. After letting him bubble for a while like a child meeting a superhero, he said: "Okay, guys, let's get down to business." He turned to Vince. "Thanks to Miss Hollie for setting up this meeting so quickly, you have the opportunity to spend one hour with my friend Phil who kindly agreed to stop here on his way to the airport. When I mentioned that Phil is one of the important people I wanted you to meet, Miss Hollie was lucky enough to find out that his team had a match here in our city yesterday."

"Wow! What a great coincidence," Vince smiled, looking at Phil.

"Actually I don't believe in coincidences," Phil said. "Anyway, let's start. As I understand it we have lots of work to do and little time to do it. So how can I help you?"

Vince explained in detail what he had learned in the last couple of days. He talked about the vision, the purpose, thinking of the team as an organization and especially of his willingness to transform all of this into tangible results—into reality.

Phil let him talk for a good five minutes, listening carefully. When Vince finished, Phil said, "Okay, now that you have your vision and mission clear, it's time to go into the more specific and concrete. Like a GPS navigation system, you know where you are.. You have your final destination and you decided the route. Now you need to identify some indicators along the way that will tell you that you're going in the right direction. One of the most important keys for success is goal setting. A good goal gives players motivation and responsibility. And when I say responsibility, I mean the real meaning of the word: the ability to respond to a particular event or environment. This is crucial for a winning team because it gives freedom to athletes. For example what is your goal for the next game?" Phil asked unexpectedly.

"Well, definitely it is not to play as we did in the last game and instead try to play better and win the match," Vince replied awkwardly.

"I'm sorry to hear that, because if you keep thinking like this, you probably will lose again!" Vince looked at him with surprise not expecting a straightforward comment like this. "First of all, if you keep focusing on what you do NOT want, that's what you will probably achieve."

"What do you mean?" Vince asked.

"Well, don't think of a purple monkey," Phil said looking straight in Vince's eyes and smiling.

"I just did as soon as you said it," Vince admitted, laughing.

"That's right. This is a basic rule of our brain: at a first level of search we don't process negations. So instead of saying that you don't want to play as badly as you did in the last game, you need to focus on what you do want. Your goals must be stated in the positive. That's the first rule!"

"Ok, I get it!" Vince corrected himself, "A good goal is 'I want my team to win the game'."

"I like your enthusiasm, but no, you didn't get it yet! That was only the first characteristic. I think you need to know more about how our brain works."

"Wow, I didn't suspect I needed to be a neurology expert to be a good coach," Vince said.

"Well, if you know the rules of your game, it's easier to win, isn't it?" Phil commented.

"That's completely true," Vince said taking out his notepad with an increasing curiosity.

"The second characteristic for a well-formed goal is that it has to be initiated and maintained by you. If you say, 'I want my team to win the game', you're not taking into account the opposing team or the referee or whatever else is not under your control and which could change the game's result."

"Are you saying that winning the game isn't a good goal?" Vince asked surprised.

"Think about winning the game as a consequence. Every season we always set goals for our team, and yes, winning is not a major goal. We feel if we can reach the majority of the goals set for every opponent we face, the winning will take care of itself. We want results. We want improvement each and every time out there. You need to have one very important question in mind: what do you expect specifically for yourself and your team or, speaking at a higher level, the organization? Which behaviors and results do your players need to express in order to win your next game?"

"So winning a game is the consequence of specific technical and tactical behaviors that allow us to create specific results," Vince summarized.

"Yes, and the goals you set need to be sensory-based. That means they must be stated in a language that the brain is designed to understand more fully. In other words, specifically what will you see, hear, and feel when you achieve your goal?"

Vince was listening carefully, but Phil wasn't sure he fully understood, so he continued, "Let me back up a bit. There are two great types of goals for you and our athletes: performance goals and process goals. Say you want to become an NBA player and win championships playing for the most important franchises until you become part of the Hall of Fame. Let's say that's your vision. This vision alone is not enough. It is your North Star and will provide direction, but as we already discussed, you need more specificity. Let's say that to live your vision, your outcome for this season is to become a first-string player on your team. That's the performance goal. In this case, you aren't comparing yourself against others. You're focusing instead on your own abilities and analyzing your performance. A typical performance goal (with that vision in mind) could be 'I want to improve my field goal percentage from .520 to .580 by the end of November.' Then we can get more specific and concrete by establishing some process goals such as 'I'll practice those shots 15 minutes every day after the training session, keeping track of my improvements. In addition, I'll do visualization work for 10 minutes every day.' These are two process goals that allow you to reach your performance goal, to get closer to your outcome goal and, later on, to live your vision."

"I like it! But what happens if I set a goal for free shooting and today the team is practicing defense?" Vince asked while thinking about different players on his team.

"Good question. That's exactly why it's important to set performance and process goals for different aspects of your game. Even if the team is practicing defense today, you can work on your concentration skills and, at the end of the session, still practice your shots. This keeps motivation alive!"

Vince was astonished. The more he talked to Phil, the more he understood that success is a matter of planning, preparation, and monitoring. "You know, even if I won a lot in the past, I never did all those things."

"I know, but now you're playing at the top level so you can't count only on your talent and you can't put your success into fate's hands. You need to train in tactics and strategies, but also in your mind. You need to know exactly where you and everybody else is going. That's the difference between a lucky season and a team that creates consistent and lasting results. Do you want to know more?"

"You bet," Vince replied firmly. "Let's go on."

"The final characteristic of a well-formed goal is that it has to be ecological."

"We must go green?" Vince joked.

"No, no," Phil laughed appreciating Vince's attitude. "It means that the goal has to maintain the quality in all your rapport systems. How will your new behaviors affect your players, your family, your coaching team, and others around you? Is there anything important to you that could go wrong if you achieve your goal? It's crucial to check this out at the beginning, so you know what to expect from others and while you're working toward your goal, you know that nothing will sabotage you."

Vince was taking notes madly. Everything was becoming clearer. It was such a blessing that Coach John had come into his life and was introducing him to such extraordinary people.

"I'm so impressed," Vince confessed. "I never thought there would be so many things to pay attention to when coaching a team."

"Well, a great coach is a leader and he needs to know how to manage people and how their brains work," Phil admitted.

"I guess I need to speak with my players so I'll understand whether they have specific goals and what those are. Then we need to look at how they can each get what they want while achieving the team goals."

"Good idea," Phil replied, laughing loudly. "And let me tell you one more thing: A great coach not only has to motivate players and lead them to outcomes. He has to teach them how to be self-motivated, how to set goals for themselves and how to achieve them. Especially when you have young players. To do this, create an action plan and make sure everybody follows it, just like a training schedule—consistent and flexible. Of course the goals and action plans for your athletes will be different than the ones for the coaching team. A good action plan contains the following," Phil counted off each one on his fingers. "It must have:

- ✓ Activities: For every goal, create a list of things that needs to be done in order to achieve the result you want.
- ✓ People in charge: Who's in charge of the listed activities? Remember that if *everybody* is accountable for something, it means that nobody will be.
- ✓ A deadline: That's when you want the single activities to be finished.
- ✓ An end result, which is the final product for every activity, and finally,
- ✓ Scheduling: For every activity, draw on your action plan the time (days/weeks/months) you need for executing it.

He continued, "Now, that's my idea of a good coach!" Phil checked his watch. "Vince, time's up. I'd love to spend extra time with you, but my flight won't wait for me. I hope I gave you some good tips." He stood up and shook Vince's hand, then turned to Coach John. "It's always a pleasure to see you John. Hope you'll come visit me when you fly to the other coast."

"You bet, my friend. Thank you again for your priceless time and help," John said.

"Hey Phil," Vince broke in. "May I take a picture with you?"

"Sure!" Phil smiled.

John took out his iPhone to immortalize this meeting of a legendary coach and a soon-to-be legendary coach.

"Please Coach John!" Vince urged. "Join us. I'd love to have a picture with both of my mentors."

He handed his phone to Miss Hollie, who smiled, knowing she was agreeing to be the official photographer for an historic night. She eagerly took three shots of one of Vince's best evenings ever.

After the farewells, Vince watched his idol walk away with class. What a great evening, he thought. He felt so grateful. New pieces of the puzzle were falling into the right places. Before going to bed that night, he wrote a text message to Coach John: "Thanks Coach, you're changing my life for the better :-)" and he attached the picture of the three of them. Then he took out his notepad and listed what he'd learned that day.

Notes to myself:

o *Setting goals is key to success*

o *There are outcome goals (for the season), performance goal (middle term), and process goal (short term)*

o *Characteristics of a well-formed goal:*

   ✓ *Stated in positive*

   ✓ *Sensory-based: what you will see, hear, and feel*

   ✓ *Initiated and maintained by you*

   ✓ *Ecological - maintains the quality of all rapport system*

o *Put the goal into action. Create an action plan with:*

   ✓ *Activities*

   ✓ *Person in charge*

   ✓ *Deadline*

   ✓ *End result*

   ✓ *Scheduling*

WHEN DO YOU START THE FUTURE ?

September 14

"Are you ready?" John was in his car looking at Vince come out of his house.

"You are obsessed with early mornings, John!" Vince said as he got in the car. "Where are you taking me today?"

After the last two days having been in different places learning different things, Vince had already figured out John's coaching plan and he liked it, although it typically meant getting up early in the morning. Although he never slept late, Vince liked his mornings to be a little slower, so he could do his morning rituals at his own pace. But this was not the time for moaning or whining. It was the time for learning.

"Today we are going somewhere different," John said. "I think you are in for a surprise!" Then as usual, he said no more and just hummed along with the radio.

Vince thought about what he'd learned yesterday and the day before and thought about how he could develop the ideas he had even further. One of the things that kept ringing in his ears was the importance of creating a joint purpose, but even more so, of creating a buy-in from the whole organization, both the players and the staff, as well as the executives. He had almost figured out what the joint purpose should be, but was still uncertain whether he should just decide and implement or whether he should create one with the key people from the various parts of the organization.

The last couple of days had been tough for Vince, as he still needed to work full time on the team and getting them ready for the next game, so he decided that he needed some direction from his new mentor, Coach John.

"John, I was thinking…" Vince said. "I need to start implementing some of these wonderful things you've given me and I need the team to see some results right now—not to mention the management and sponsors—otherwise they're going to come to get me!"

"Let's talk about that in the car on the way home. We are almost where we want to be!"

Vince looked out the window searching for anything that remotely resembled a sports arena, but all he could see were business buildings of the grander scale as far as the eye could see.

"Today we're going to visit a very special friend of mine and he's kindly set aside one hour this morning, and that's more than he gives his wife in a day!" John laughed at his own remark and you could clearly tell he was excited about the forthcoming meeting. Vince went along with John and got excited even though he had no clue what he was getting excited about.

They pulled up in front of a very elegant building. Vince recognized the name of the company. He was surprised, but he got even more excited although he had absolutely no idea what this could bring, if anything at all. But he trusted Coach John and for that reason he raced along as John strode into the reception area where the receptionist was opening up the company for the day. She looked up and smiled.

"Mr. Craft, what a pleasant surprise!" She smiled genuinely. "And who is your guest? He looks familiar."

"Alice, this is Vince Longman, I'm sure he needs no further introduction. Is Jack in?"

Alice laughed. "Are you kidding me, he has been in at least an hour already. Sometimes I wonder if he ever goes home. He needs someone to tell him to relax or he'll wear himself out one day soon!"

John smiled and laughed. "I think Jack is old enough to take care of himself and, by the way, when you reach a certain age, you don't need to sleep so much. You will find out when you get older."

They both laughed hard and Vince could tell they knew each other quite well. Alice looked like she was in her sixties too, so the joke was the sort that old friends would use or of course true gentlemen, but there was something else. Vince made a promise to ask John when they got back in the car.

Alice called someone on the phone and two minutes later another lady about the same age as Alice showed up. "Coach John, so good to see you again. It's been a while!"

"Yes it has, hasn't it? And you haven't grown a day older since I saw you last. What do you eat? I need to get some!" Again the laugh and Vince had a feeling that these were all old friends of Coach John, but he failed to connect the dots.

They took the elevator up to the sixth floor and got out. No doubt that they were on the executive floor of a very successful operation. The secretary escorted them to a room large enough to hold two families. A side door opened and in came a man who instantly filled the whole room with his presence. Others would describe both Vince and Coach John this same way, but this was different. Vince had to admit that he was a bit intimidated while he was still getting warmed up in the big leagues. But he also had to admit that if there was anybody who should be allowed to intimidate him, then this person was sure the right one.

"John, thank you for coming! And Vince Longman . . . I've heard so much about you. Judging from the reports I've gotten, I believe you can become what John was in his sport!"

Vince was speechless. This man knew so much about him and thought so highly of him, but he was the rookie head coach in the league. And why did he thank Coach John for coming? Shouldn't it be the other way round?

John could tell Vince was out of words so he interrupted, "Well, hopefully bigger and hopefully a lot faster than me. It took me forever to find out the secrets, so we're fast-tracking Vince, so he can be a whole lot more."

Jack and John laughed, and Jack said, "Well, both you and I had to crawl on some virgin territory. We sure have had our ups and downs, but in the long run, we proved it could be done and that our way is the right one. Let's sit down!"

They sat down and Jack looked at Vince. "So why are you a Head Coach?"

Vince looked at him. "I'm the Head Coach because the team needs someone who keeps the overview and connects the dots and keeps the ship sailing in the right direction. I'm there to direct and support my coaching staff and players, especially the Team Captains!

"Good" Jack said. "So why do you have a team?"

Vince didn't reply immediately as he wasn't sure what Jack meant. So he tried his luck and said, "If you don't mind me asking, sir, what would be your idea of why we are a team?"

Jack struck up a loud laugh. "He's good John. He's good." He was laughing so much that tears started running out of his eyes. "Well, I tell you this son, you got guts and in my little tiny world that means a lot. I'll answer your question, but not before you tell me what you've got because, if I am not mistaken, you already have a purpose written out in your head, don't you?"

Vince, surprised at how this man could see right through him, said, "I'm still not sure about the final phrasing and whether I should create it along with the rest of the key people, but what I have so far goes like this: *The purpose of the team is to develop and nurture a championship organization that can go all the way.* What do you think about that, sir?"

"Two things. When you come here as a friend of Coach John, I am 'Jack' and not 'sir.' I do appreciate you being well-mannered, but I am Jack, okay?" Vince nodded and Jack continued, "I think you got it, or at least it's very close, and I think you can create it, but make sure you know how to explain it and create buy-in when you sit down with the ambassadors who have to spread it! A good purpose is the fundamental understanding of why we exist. It's as important as a good clear vision and it helps you navigate, to stay inside your own metaphor. You may want to add something about supporting each other in the pursuit and then consider defining what all that means. But I'll leave that up to you. You seem smart enough to figure it out yourself. Now, if we shift a little bit of our focus and look at the organization you're a part of, as with the purpose statement, successful organizations in both business and sports have a mindset of strategic thinking and long-term planning. This means defining goals for the future, not just for this year, but also for the next year and the next."

Jack looked straight at Vince and continued, "Try for a moment this little exercise: I don't know what ultimate result you're dreaming about, but in the dream world everything is possible. What are you trying to make or achieve? What excites and inspires you about it? If you could wave a magic wand and do anything you like, what would you create? Using your imagination, just think about it. Go to that particular experience that would tell you that you're there. Imagine it as if you are fully into the situation, taking part in it as if you're really there, with all the commotion going on around you. Notice how it looks, notice how it sounds and notice how it feels being there. Notice also when it is happening, is it one, two, three, four or five years from now? Go to ten years from now, if you can. Now imagine you're watching all of this from above, as if you're filming it from a blimp hovering above and then ask yourself, do you want this? My guess is that the answer is yes. The next step is to ask yourself what resources you need to make this happen: people, money, materials and technology? What's your plan? What obstacles will you face? How will you get around them? Imagine the future as a line in front of you. Mark out the present moment in front of you and then start thinking about the things you would like to happen for your team this year and then next year and then the next year, and notice how you'd like the team to evolve over, let's say, the next five or ten years. When you look at the things you would like to happen, you know that there are things that have to happen in order to make that happen, don't you?"

Vince nodded as he was sitting with his eyes closed, imagining the future in the way he would like it to be.

Jack continued, "Now if you think of that sequence of events as your timeline, you can then extend and re-orient things in a way that fits your purpose. But let me ask you, what do you see out there and how far away from the now is it?"

Vince, still with his eyes closed, looked at the horizon of his vision and said, "It's pretty far away and I see great things, but I don't want it to be just a short-lived success. I want it to be a sustainable future, where we, year after year, can come back and play the game we want to play and dictate the field. I see us becoming the greatest organization in sports ever, the one everyone wants to be part of, and if they can't, then the one they try to copy." His voice had a thick sound to it and he said it with emotions so clear and present that the two other men in the room could tell that he truly believed and that his passion for the sport and the team was indeed pure and coming from the bottom of his heart.

For a moment no one said anything, but after a while, Jack said, "Vince, when you keep looking at that amazing future for your team, what kind of players do you see out there, who are making all of this happen?"

Vince sat for a while and from his facial expression you could tell he was in debate with himself. "I see a completely different team. Some of the players are the same, but many are gone and many new faces have appeared. The team looks happier and they look like a team!" The last remark was said in a different tone of voice, as if Vince had just realized something important.

He opened his eyes and said, "I think I know what's been bothering me ever since I got here. I'm not sure I have the solution to my own question, but we don't look like a team and it has to do with certain players not playing for the team. They're the stars, but in reality, they play their own game so much that it hurts the morale of the new talented kids we have and the older players who are still committed with blood and soul to this organization."

Vince just stared into the room as if no one else was there and as if he had just had a revelation!

"So let me ask you something, Vince. What do you think I would do here on my team if I had people who acted like you just described?"

"You would probably just fire them and get new ones, but we have different conditions. We can't hire new players mid-season and we need the stars. They attract the fans and media and, without them, we wouldn't be able to play at this level!"

"How many do you have that can step up if needed?" Jack asked.

Jack looked at Vince and Vince looked back. Then he replied, "As you know I just took over this team in the spring before the new season and I really don't have that many that I can move up. We would get our asses beaten so badly that we'd lose all our fans and sponsors. I don't think that alternative is a very attractive one."

"You're probably right. You better let the mavericks run the team the way they do because you play great right now!"

The sarcasm in Jack's voice was unmistakably harsh and Vince gazed back at him, grasping the harsh reality.

"You know, I think I'm getting what you're saying. Not sure I understand what to do or if I like what's implicated in that answer, but I do understand! You're telling me that if I keep the current team, we will play badly anyway and still not get the future I dream of, so it is only a matter of priority when I want to start building that future!"

For a while no one in the room said anything. Vince's last words were hovering in the room and the consequences of having said them were not attractive, but Vince was relieved in a way. He knew what had to be done, but still had no clue of how.

BUILDING LONG TERM SUCCESS

In the car on the way back to the clubhouse, Vince sat for a long time without saying anything. He was just sitting looking out the windshield almost as if he didn't know that Coach John was also in the car.

Suddenly he said, "John may I ask you a personal question?" He waited and when John didn't deny him the opportunity, he continued "It seemed like to me that you knew his secretary very well... am I wrong?"

John laughed "Well let's just say that I have also gone to college..." He smiled with a warm smile "Alice was a cheerleader and... well we dated for a while and we were a good couple... but my sports and her studies required us both to move to different places in the country and we broke up, but in a friendly manor, we will always have a special place in each other's hearts. She by the way was the one connecting me and Jack!" John disappeared for a while into memory lane and drove on with the warm smile on his face, leaving Vince to think and reflect.

After a while Vince broke the silence "You know what John? This whole thing is a bit scary!"

John nodded. He knew what Vince meant. He had been there himself and knew the price was high and that only the toughest would survive. John decided not to say anything right away and to let Vince find answers in his own mind. John never doubted for a second that Vince was tough enough to do what was necessary, but Vince needed to realize this for himself.

Back at the clubhouse, they had lunch but didn't talk much. John decided he would leave Vince for the rest of the day, allowing him to reflect on his possible solutions. John decided it was time to call for backup and left Vince to find a quiet place where he could make this important call.

******

"Gentlemen, I have gathered you on short notice, because I want to speak openly with you all on a very grave matter!" Vince looked at his coaching staff. It was a very diverse bunch of people and as good as any assistant coach staff. "I deeply respect each and every one of you and I also respect your honest opinions. That's why I've called you all to this meeting. This morning, I realized that we cannot allow our team to continue in the way we're doing things right now. I don't have the solution, but would like all of you to contribute your own ideas about what we could do to change, not just the attitudes, but also the behaviors of this team."

The assistant coaches looked at Vince, but no one said anything, until Dumbbell Jack started. "Well you know, Vince, I respect you a lot, because I know what you've accomplished in your short career, but I think you're wasting your time running around with Coach John. You should be here and not everywhere else and then you should be more aggressive with the players. That is, if you ask me."

"Thank you, Jack. It's certainly a piece of advice. How about the rest of you guys?"

One by one, the coaches came up with their ideas, most of which had to do with Vince being more firm and aggressive in order to build in the players a state of almost fear for the Head Coach. Vince had always hated that approach. He considered it old-fashioned and he had hated it as a player and as a young assistant coach. He didn't say anything, however. He just listened, but he started thinking about whether the transition should be only players or if he also needed to make radical adjustments to the whole organization around the team. How much turmoil can the team handle? he asked himself.

After the meeting, he called Coach John. "John, I've just had a meeting with my assistant coaches on what ideas they have about the team and the situation. Quite frankly, their suggestions were not the ones I was looking for and it made me think. Do you have time for dinner tonight? I have something I'd like to discuss with you."

At the other end of the line John smiled. Here was a young man who was about to move somewhere and he was now starting to reclaim the initiative!

*****

They had picked a restaurant where they could sit and talk without other people hearing them. Vince was eager to get started and almost didn't touch his food. John felt like he was behaving like an old parent when he said, "Vince, eat your food. You need the energy." He laughed and Vince politely took a bite of his steak, but he had every intention of getting right down to business.

"Coach, meeting your friend Jack and then having the meeting with my assistant coach staff this afternoon has made me realize that something drastic has to happen. I need to make a complete rebuild. That means this whole season could end up being the worst in the team's history. We'll lose fans and sponsors, so I am bit concerned about the scale of my thoughts. When I look at what I want to accomplish with this team and why I was took the Head Coach position, the crew and the target don't match up." He looked at John and continued, "I'm not even sure if Mr. R will accept something so drastic. I know he thinks the world of me, but he also has an investment to take care of!"

"Well, as you say, it's an investment and, yes, some people invest to make a short-term gain, but others invest more long-term. You can buy a player who can step right into the team and perform and in sports you sometimes have to do that because of injury or if a player gets a better offer from another team. But the more you plan for the future, the less you have to panic when that happens because you have the material that can step up and replace, making it an organic organization. That's what a good business does and that's what a powerhouse of a sports club does! I don't think Mr. R is in this for the short-term gain, but when you're ready and have a plan, I think you should ask him personally. In the meantime, since we're here and your steak seems like it will last the whole evening with the pace you're eating it, I want to ask you something else. Meanwhile, I'll have the cheesecake I saw on the dessert cart. Yummy, it just looked so good and will be a good supplement to my diet."

Coach John laughed so much at his own joke that he almost fell off the chair and Vince admired John for being able to keep his sense of humor. It was almost as if no problem was too big to be laughed at and Vince knew that this was part of Coach John's legacy: his ability to laugh at things while working on something as if it is the most important thing in the world.

With the look of a child with candy in his mouth, John chewed his cheesecake. He had convinced the waiter that he should have an especially big slice as it would be the last in his life. The waiter had taken this as a wish from a man dying and had sliced him a quarter of the cake. John was truly pleased with himself and it could be seen on his face.

He wiped the crumbs off his mouth and said, "Vince, you've primarily worked with teams where you've had to work with what you were given, but thinking about the future you described this morning, you may have to do things very differently. What's your experience with planning players, not just for the season, but also thinking strategic planning of players? Have you heard about a Belgium guy called Paul Ponnet?" John asked.

Vince shook his head.

"Well, Paul is a friend of mine and he's developed a system for talent development. In short, it's about how you nurture talent and make sure that you move them one step at a time, but with a long-term scope. Allow me briefly to explain his approach. Having long-term success in any sport requires dedication, focus, planning and patience. It can work in any size organization around a team or group of individuals and should, of course, be customized to fit your organization and its particulars. The purpose of the system is to help the staff and organization around the team, the athletes, to detect, develop and manage talent. Talent here is broadly defined, but generally speaking, looking at the athletes who will ensure results in a three- to five-year timeframe. The method is not a quick fix, but rather a long-term solution that will enable the organization to build talent that can support results over time. In many cases, results will start to show quickly, but that isn't the main focus, just a byproduct of doing the right thing."

"So what you're saying is that it's a system that supports the vision I described this morning?" Vince interrupted.

John nodded then continued, "The system requires dedication to long-term thinking and it requires discipline from the involved staff members, whose patience may be challenged if they can only focus on short-term results. The process works with both structures and methods for dealing, not only with technical, tactical and physical skills but also, equally important, with the mindsets of the staff and athletes. There are five phases to the process."

Vince sensed something important coming and quickly grabbed his notebook and a pen and kept listening as John continued the explanation.

"This system is even more about the coaching staff and their approaches, but also needs to be thoroughly explained to the players. You need to recruit a new kind of player who is willing to wait for big results, but who also is committed long-term to bigger, better and more rewarding results. There are a lot of details in how you work with the individual athlete, but for now, I would like to just focus on the phases that involve the mindsets of the coaching staff. Phase one: First, you examine the current practices and mindsets of the coaching staff, but also in the athletes you have. So the goal is to get a snapshot of complete potential in the staff and the current group of athletes. In this first phase, you'll examine carefully the staff involved in handling the talent. This includes senior administrative staff involved in decision-making around the dispositions of the athletes."

Vince made a note and then looked up.

John continued, "Phase two is about designing the short- and long-term support processes that you need to set up so that nothing drops through the floor. You need to plan it so that everyone in the organization can see the benefit for them. In other words – what's in it for them?"

Vince nodded and said, "So the goal of this phase is alignment and buy-in of the steps for progress."

John smiled at how quickly Vince was getting the ideas he was presenting and added, "The second phase will be designed and based on the findings during phase one. Although the process and method is generic, each organization and each sport has its own particulars to be taken into consideration and all of this will result in the initial process chart that will outline steps to be taken on short-, medium- and long-term. For this team, I think we should look at a three-year plan at first. In the third phase, you need to train the involved staff in the agreed structures and methods, so that everyone has the knowledge and understanding of how the system works. Here, the goal is that each trainer and staff member involved in the process should be able to develop, handle and support the athletes accordingly. They don't need to know everything at once, so it would be recommended to take it in steps as the system unfolds, so that they can focus on what they have to focus on while building skills and gaining experience."

Vince smiled. "I really like this approach. Of course, I need to know more and perhaps meet this friend of yours, but so far it meshes with my beliefs!"

John, already knowing this last piece of information, continued his explanation. "The tough part is phase four, when the staff starts implementing the system. This is when obstacles and challenges happen. The system may need more customization, to fit, and of course the challenge here is to keep everyone believing in the system and motivated to continue, even when there are potential setbacks!"

"I know!" Vince said. "I've tried changing playing styles before and know how much of a struggle it can be when the results are not coming in game one. I can only imagine that with a complete revamp of systems and methods for player development and what that brings, how much there can be to combat once we say go."

John nodded with a serious look on his face. "Yes, this approach is not for the weak-hearted. It requires guts at a level that few have, but the few who do have been rewarded and have never looked back. And then, of course, as with all other changes, it requires follow-up throughout the whole process!"

Vince nodded and made more notes. He looked up and straight into John's eyes. "I like it! I want to do it! I need to talk to Mr. R and get his support for this plan. It is precisely aligned with what your friend Jack talked about this morning and it is exactly aligned with my thinking and ambition for this team and club!"

Notes to myself:
- ✓ *Think long-term*
- ✓ *Have a purpose and a vision for the future*
- ✓ *If you can dream it, you can do it*
- ✓ *Set the right team on and off the field*
- ✓ *Examine current practices and mindsets*
- ✓ *Design the short- and long-term support process*
- ✓ *Train the involved staff in the agreed structures and methods*
- ✓ *Support for agreed structures and methods*
- ✓ *Follow up*

AM I IMPORTANT ?

Vince had emailed Mr. R the night before and was anxiously waiting for his request for a meeting. He now knew what had to be done, but he also remembered the advice, both from his Coaching Idol Phil and from his meeting yesterday with the businessman Jack. "Where are you?" It kept ringing in his head as if there was something he had overlooked. He really shouldn't be concerned with this right now as today was game day and he had tons of things on his mind, but once Vince had committed to something, there was no turning back. That was his situation as he entered the clubhouse and went to the locker rooms to address the team before the game.

He had met with the coaching staff the night before and he had asked each and every one of them their honest opinion about each player, their game plan, and all the aspects of the game, as well as the motivational status of the team. He had mapped out where he believed they were so that he had a better picture of, not just of where he wanted to go, but also where he was coming from.

The latter was something he had not done before. He had been so busy looking in the direction he wanted to go, that he had not been concerned about where he was coming from—where he was starting his journey. It made a lot of sense that this also had to be considered in order to assess how to get where you wanted to go, but things had never been so complex before and the level of stakeholders was very different now. He had realized this late, but not too late.

Once inside the locker room, he saw the usual sight before a game. Everyone was in their own pregame trance, trying to get ready for the game. Each player had their own ritual to perform. Purely superstition, but Vince would be the last person to interfere with that. He even had his own ritual before leaving home.

He had thought a lot about how to address the players. They needed a win badly after last week's total collapse, but Vince was uncertain about how much of his new knowledge was supposed to be short-term. On the way into the basement, he had finally decided that he would start using the purpose statement as a guideline for the combined effort.

He looked around in the locker room and found his usual spot. For some reason, he preferred to be at the exact same spot and he actually would go far to find a similar spot when they were playing away games. This was the second part of his ritual and every little detail counted. He always took a minute to gather his thoughts, to think back to his favorite coach and a particular pep talk he had given before a very important game. It was a good strong anchor for him and as soon as that moment was over, he asked one of the players to yell out for all the players to huddle up around him.

"Gentlemen, as you know we have a lot to prove today and I am not talking about our fans in the stadium, our sponsors or the many people watching at home on their television. No, I'm talking about proving to ourselves that we are a team, that we are made out of the right material, that we have what it takes and that we have the strengths to climb back up on the horse. Yes, we were thrown off the horse last week, but our determination, our stamina, our will to win should be obvious to each and every one watching and to each and every one of us playing today. Are you guys ready to rumble?"

All the players yelled out loudly that they were ready and then continued with their pregame rituals. Vince felt that he had conveyed the message right and he hoped this would be the turning point of this team.

******

The game was a tough game. No doubt that Vince's team had entered the field to prove something, but the opposing team, also with a recent defeat, was not visiting to lose. Vince could tell that he had managed to inspire his players, at least in the beginning of the game. Every passage was smooth and precise, the entire team was synchronized. Everything was flowing. Vince was in the game with his team: he was giving direction, calling plays, running and screaming on the sideline. He knew he was going to make it and it felt so great. Everything was working perfectly.

He was so happy that he didn't see it coming. It was like a thunderbolt: quick, but dramatically powerful.

Steve "Old Guy" Tyler, the oldest and one of the more trustful players Vince had in the team, was looking to throw deep down in the open field. Two players ran against him to sack him or steal the ball while James Larson, with a very smart and unpredictable move, was good enough to run and place himself alone in the middle of the open field, ready to score: he just needed the ball. They looked each other with understanding. James smiled. He knew he could score.

But something went wrong. Old Guy turned his face and decided to keep the ball to try the impossible. Everybody was shocked. Time slowed while he ran the ball. From the sideline, Vince wasn't breathing as his eyes followed Tyler and the ball. He found himself praying for Tyler to hang onto the ball. The slow time was brutally broken when one hand caught Tyler's arm. Unfortunately, it wasn't a friendly hand. Lee Davis, the opposing team's best defensive player, intercepted the ball and started running in the opposite direction. Most of Vince's players were still shocked and totally unprepared for what was happening: a big counterattack. They were caught with their pants down and seemed stiff and unable to move.

Perception of time changed dramatically: now it was very fast. Vince's team tried to get back and defend, but it was too late. The other team scored!

Vince was petrified. He couldn't believe it. His most trusted player just betrayed him. Why in the hell didn't Old Guy Tyler pass that ball? James was alone. He could have easily scored and put an important seal on the match. Instead he decided to try by himself.

Now the pressure was tremendously high. Vince could feel his veins pushing against his temples. He breathed deeply and brought more oxygen to his brain. He needed to be calm and think. They could still make it.

Vince looked at the players on the field and noticed that Hack Hampor, one of the youngest and most talented players, was running around quite confused because of what had just happened. He decided to take him out on the sidelines, without putting more pressure on him, and started shouting to the others in order to reorganize the game.

After fifteen minutes, Hack was still confused and when he re-entered the game, he missed an easy play that, luckily for the team, was not picked up by the opponents.

Vince knew at that moment that he needed to change something. He looked at the replacements and there it was: Bob Fisher. In his mid-thirties, Bob was the team's most experienced player. Having played in the pros a few years longer than Old Guy made him one of the reference points on the team.

Even if Orlando Jives tried to discourage Vince from keeping Bob because of his age and possible injuries, Vince wanted Bob because he could be a great teacher and a very positive influence for the young Hack and eventually helpful during hard times. And this was the hardest time.

"Fisher, you're going in," Vince said.

The player needed just a couple of minutes to warm up because he had already started by himself, eager to help out.

Before going on the field, he walked by Vince and said in a weird tone of voice, "It's about time. You will not regret this, Coach," and he went in, very focused.

Vince looked at Bob and replayed the weird comment in his head, but he immediately focused again on the match, hoping it was the right move.

In an unpredictable turn of events, Bob took the ball and started drawing perfect lines and schemes. He took the team by the hand and all his teammates once again started a good game and they began scoring.

Vince's team won the game. They didn't play their best game, but luckily this obstacle was overcome. While going towards the locker room, Fisher was laughing and hugging his teammates. Thank God, Vince had done the right thing, but something deep inside was still not right.

After the press conference, Vince went to his office and found Coach John waiting for him.

"Good comeback tonight," John began.

"Yes. Luckily Bob was in the zone. He played a great game," Vince commented.

John noticed that something was going on in Vince's mind. "Son, you don't seem totally satisfied. Are you?"

"It's not that I'm not satisfied, but something I didn't expect happened on the field tonight and I'm learning to pay attention to these alarms. This time we won, so everything is okay, but I didn't like what happened and it worries me." Then Vince explained the comment Bob Fisher made before going on the field and his astonishment about Old Guy Tyler's play.

"Mmmmhhhh, you have two great points here!" Coach John commented. "First of all, congratulations! Most people would have let those things go because they won, but in the long run, this situation could lead to defeat. My dear Vince, this is a great opportunity to practice some skills."

Smiling, Coach John picked up the phone and said, "Okay, Miss Hollie, set the appointment for tomorrow morning at 8.30."

"It looks like you already know what needs to be done," Vince said smiling.

"Well, I'm here for this reason," John replied laughing. "But before thinking about tomorrow, we need to talk a little more about what happened today. In the last few days, you learned that, in order to have a great team and organization, you need to have a clear Purpose, a Vision, and Values that will guide the team to achieve some specific Goals you set. And of course you need to plan strategically and create an effective action plan. Now you only need to put the right people in the right place to do the right thing."

Vince, looking confused, said, "Well, every player already knows what to do. I'm very detailed. We have three to five video sessions every week. I explain all the plays during the week and we rehearse every day. I also give them a memo of what they are supposed to do in almost every second of the game so that they can study it at home."

"That's really good," Coach John said, "but I'm not talking only about the game and the play. I'm talking about their role in the team."

Vince looked even more confused. "They already know their roles. What are you talking about?"

"I told you, it's not only about the game," Coach John said firmly. "It's about the team! Let me give you an example: why did you choose to keep Bob Fisher when you formed the team?"

"Well, because he's experienced and he could be a good role model for the young athletes," Vince answered. "If only Hack Hampor could get some of his skills and attitude, we would be okay for the next ten years. I mean, Bob's the perfect player who can resolve any situation—like he did tonight."

"But he wants to play," John said.

"Every player wants to play," Vince replied.

Coach John looked at Vince. "Well, both yes and no! 'Yes' because when you are a top athlete and you compete at this level, you want to show everybody what you can do and achieve the best result. But 'No' if you know what you were chosen and are paid for a particular role that does not necessarily require playing time on the same level as everybody else!"

"Tell me more," Vince was becoming more and more curious.

"Let's say, for example, that at the beginning of the season you talked to Bob and told him that his main role for the season was to mentor and nurture Hack, teaching him everything he could. And maybe a big part of his bonuses were attached to how well he performed this task and to Hack's improvements."

"I get your point," Vince opened his eyes. "Today Bob would have never commented that way and probably he would have supported Hack from the beginning!"

"That's right. And what about having for every player and member of the coaching staff a job description with the specific role and what you expect from them? When everybody knows the common goals set for the team and what role each member is supposed to play, you are guiding every effort and minimizing the risk of conflicts. In the end, this leads to victory and lasting success." Coach John paused and looked at Vince.

"Nothing is left to chance, is it?" Vince commented smiling.

"Johnny Carson once said: 'Talent alone won't make you a success. Neither will being in the right place at the right time, unless you are ready.' The most important question is 'Are you ready'?"

"During the past week, I think I've learned more about how to be prepared than I have during the last two years."

"Good, now let's address the second point. If you were a player like Old Guy Tyler, why you would choose to keep the ball and not to pass it to the team star who was alone in the middle of the field and could easily score?"

"Well, I would have never done it!" Vince immediately replied.

"Yes, you probably wouldn't have. But you didn't answer my question. You need to think like Old Guy. Put yourself in his shoes for a while and tell me what would make you do that," Coach John said firmly.

"Mmmmmhhh, probably I would do that if I think I can score by myself!"

"And why would you want to score by yourself when you know there is a teammate better positioned than you?"

"Because I want to score."

"And when do YOU want to score, risking not making it instead of passing the ball and being sure that the team will make it?"

"When I want all the fans to shout my name, when I want my teammates to be grateful, when I want the coach to trust me, when I need to do something special. Wait a minute!" Vince was staring at John. "It's when I don't feel significant enough and I want to show that I'm important for the team."

"Bingo!" John replied smiling and continued, "Many of those behaviors happen when the need of significance is not fulfilled."

"The need of significance?" Vince repeated.

"Yes. It's one of the most important human needs. We all have it and we can fulfill it in different ways. Especially in a team sport, where the group is above all the single components, you want to make sure that everybody has this need fulfilled. And you can do it through your decisions about who's playing or not, through prizes, through bonuses or simply through your words in a press conference or in the locker room… there are so many ways to fulfill it, but you want to be aware of what's going on and calibrate the level of satisfaction in regards to this need in your team members."

Vince was staring at Coach John thinking how many things he still needed to learn to be a good coach.

"Remember: there is no 'I' in team, but it doesn't mean that you have to forget the individuals. If you don't make them feel important, they will do everything they can in order to emerge from the team and achieve their own significance. And sometimes they will do stupid things like what we saw tonight."

"That rings a bell," Vince commented. "So if I agree with every player and member of the coaching staff on a specific role, not only on the field but also outside, and I make sure—every now and then—that everybody feels important and significant for the team, I can actually have people without weird expectations and who are fighting with every fiber of their soul for the greatest good."

"You got it!" Coach John said proudly. "Now let's go home and get some rest. It has been a very long day and tomorrow we will add some other skills in order to be even more ready." Laughing they exited the office like two old friends up to something really exciting.

As soon as Vince got home, practicing his new good habits so he would have everything clear in his mind, he took the notepad and wrote what he learned during the day:

Notes to myself:

- ✓ *In order to get where you want to be, you need to know where you are*

- ✓ *Set a team role for each member of the group: i.e., nurture and mentor the youngest, monitoring the emotional state of the team, etc.*

- ✓ *Pay attention to the need of significance. Smart people can do stupid things when they feel they're not important. Fulfill this need with decisions, prizes, words, roles, putting in charge, etc.*

- ✓ *Make sure their expectations match your goals and plans.*

THE ART OF FEEDBACK

September 15

Vince arrived at the stadium fifteen minutes before the appointment, so he decided to have a cup of coffee in the bar. When he entered, a familiar voice called to him.

"Vince!"

"Hey, Coach John! Are you already here?" Vince greeted his mentor.

"Yes, I go with the Lombardi time," replied John shaking his hand.

"Lombardi time? What's that?" Vince sensed that the first lesson of the day had already started in these few seconds.

"Well, the great Hall of Fame football coach of the Green Bay Packers, Vince Lombardi, invented a strategy that he recommended to his coaches and players. It came to be known as 'Lombardi Time' and it embodied a valuable habit. Lombardi Time states: 'Show up for every important meeting fifteen minutes ahead of the scheduled time.' The idea is to use the fifteen minutes to catch your breath, collect your thoughts, and start focusing on what you want to accomplish in the meeting and how you'll go about it. In this way, you're practicing being ahead of the game." Coach John laughed in the style he always used when he said something casual, but important.

After breakfast, they got in John's car together, ready for the upcoming day. As it would take 45 minutes to reach their destination, Vince decided it would be a great time for asking Coach John a question that had been hammering Vince's mind for a couple of days.

"John, can I ask you a question?"

"You just did!" John replied smiling and then he continued, "Yes, sure you can."

"What do you think about Jack Keshigan, our physical coach?" Vince hoped to discover the reason for Dumbbell Jack's dislike towards John.

"I think he's one of the best physical coaches in the league, very well prepared!" John answered while he kept looking straight ahead.

Vince knew that if he wanted answers, he needed to ask precise questions. "I've noticed that he's not your biggest supporter. If you don't mind that I ask, did something happen when you worked together in the past?" Vince asked directly with a bit of embarrassment in his voice.

"Actually, yes. I threw him off the team," Coach John replied in a neutral tone of voice.

"You just said that he's one of the best physical coaches. Wasn't he doing a good job at the time?" Vince asked trying to find the answer.

"No, he was doing an excellent job. I was very impressed!" John said.

Now Vince looked very confused. "Excuse me. If he was doing an excellent job, why did you throw him off the team?"

"Very simple. He wasn't aligned with the team." John answered calmly.

"What do you mean? He wasn't working toward the same goals?" Vince was becoming more interested.

"You've learned the importance of goal setting. If it's significant for an athlete, it's also crucial for a team. Sharing a goal, a result, a methodology or whatever, means you need to know it, approve it and, above all, behave in the way you agreed. But, as you perfectly well know already, when you communicate your ideas to a team, some people won't necessarily agree with you. So what would you do in this case?" John asked.

"I would probably try to explain why my point of view is better than theirs," Vince replied.

"Yes, until it comes to a point when you have to make a decision. Here comes the 'alignment' which means to behave in the way we decided without necessarily agreeing with everything. This little difference between 'total agreement' and 'alignment' is a key factor for long-term results. When the team members are not aligned, perhaps they can achieve some results in the short run, but they will fail in the long run, because during difficult times everybody will go in different directions... but the boat is always the same one. Alignment requires growth and team spirit. There's a time when you can discuss and try to make your point and change someone else's mind but then, if you can't persuade the other person, you need to define a common line and pursue it."

"If you can't be the sun, don't be the cloud," Vince commented.

"That's right!" Coach John nodded. "Especially if results don't arrive immediately, you shouldn't fall into the trap of 'I told you so!' That only generates bad feelings and conflicts. On a team that works well together, everybody can share their ideas. And if I can't persuade others of my point of view, my point of view must be the same of the team. That's why Jack was kicked off the team. He was doing a great job, but when the moment of supporting a specific team decision came up, he said 'I don't agree with that and I know that others don't either, but the majority decided to do it and so we're forced to.' At that very moment I was beginning to build a team so I couldn't afford to have a close staff member who behaved like that, even if he was the top in his field."

Vince was thinking how much guts it would take to make certain decisions. "Have you ever cut an important player because he wasn't aligned?" Vince finally asked.

"Yes, once. He was the star player of my team in 1984. I still remember the moment. His name was Phil... Phil Larson." John looked at Vince.

"Larson? That's funny, the same last name as..." The smile on Vince's face disappeared as he realized who this Phil was: James's dad!

"Yes, Phil Larson, the dad of one of your best players and he too was a remarkable player. He hated me for a few years afterwards, but in the end he thanked me for what I did, because he had a serious wakeup call after that episode. He thought he was untouchable, that he could walk on water, but one day he woke up realizing he couldn't and that he was wet up to his neck. We're actually quite good friends today and talk regularly. I probably could have told him in a nicer way that he was on his way out, but I gave it to him directly in his face. If there's one thing in my career I regret, perhaps it was the way I cut him, but I was younger and still learning. By the way, that's the reason for today's field trip. Today I'm going to introduce you to one of the best communicators in sports. His name is Andrew Hawk. He replaced Phil Larson and became the captain of my team for three years before becoming head coach on his own. Andrew wasn't the best player, but he was the best leader I've ever had and all his teammates loved him for his exceptional way of communicating. You will love learning from him."

"I always thought I had good communication skills," Vince said honestly.

"Yes, you do and that's why I want you to go to the next level. I called him up asking if he would share some of his secrets with you."

"That sounds interesting. What do you want me to watch?" Vince asked.

"Actually I don't want you to watch. I want you to listen carefully. Notice the words, the voice tone and inflection."

At that moment, they arrived at the arena.

"Hi, Andrew! How're you doing?"

"Hi, Coach John! Nice to see you on the field again!" Andrew said.

John laughed. "No, no. I'm here because I want to introduce you to my dear friend, Vince Longman." The two men shook hands. "And I'd love if you could spend some time with him explaining something about your communication style."

"Sure! I have a meeting in ten minutes with one of my players because I want to give him feedback about something he should have done yesterday, but didn't. So, Vince, come with me and instead of explaining it, I will show you."

Vince, feeling like a fish out of water, replied, "Hold on. I don't feel it's right to attend a private session with one of your players, especially if you need to give him negative feedback."

"Don't worry," Andrew laughed. "First of all, there is no positive or negative feedback: feedback is feedback. You want to put a positive intention behind it. That's what will create change. Second, on my team, we all have the feedback culture. This is the first thing I instill."

"What's a feedback culture?" Vince asked.

"Well, it's very simple and powerful." Andrew took a flipchart and drew a matrix.

	KNOWN TO SELF	UNKNOWN TO SELF
KNOWN TO OTHERS	OPEN	BLIND
UNKNOWN TO OTHERS	HIDDEN	UNKNOWN

"This is called a Johari Window and it's a tool to help people better understand their relationship with self and others. I don't use it as a psychological tool, but I teach it to my players because it gives a clear representation of what can happen when you improve your communication."

Vince looked puzzled "What do you mean by 'improve your communication'?"

"It's very simple. As you can see in the figure, there are four windows: Window one is the part of ourselves that we see and others see. It's called OPEN area and it's that part of our conscious self – our attitudes, behavior, motivation, values, way of life – of which we are aware and which is known to others. We move within this area with freedom, we are 'open books'."

Vince nodded to show that he understood and made some notes in his book.

Andrew continued, "Window two is the aspect that others see, but we are not aware of. Maybe with my words, I judge people around me, but I don't realize it because I've always done it that way. This is called BLIND area, because we each have a blind spot we can't see. There are things about ourselves that we don't know, but that others can see more clearly. Or things we imagine to be true of ourselves for a variety of reasons, but that others do not see at all."

"Window three is our private space, which we know but keep from others. It's the HIDDEN area and men, especially, tend to keep it secret most of the time. Finally, we have window four which is the most mysterious room, where the unconscious part of us is seen by neither ourselves nor others. It's the UNKNOWN area and here lies our undeveloped potential."

"That's very interesting, but I still can't get how it can improve our team communication."

"Well, the challenge is to amplify your OPEN area. The more you're an open book on the team, the easier it gets for the team to work with you and for you to work with the team."

"Yes, that's clear. A larger open area means more accountability and less misunderstanding. How can we expand that pane?"

"Good question! The secret is this: disclosure and feedback."

"Disclosure and feedback?"

"Yes. Or simply telling and asking. Let's say for example that you had a very bad day. You argued with your son, the bank didn't give you a loan, someone stupid scratched your car door, etc. and you arrive in that state to the training session. Maybe some of your players start joking around and after a while, you scream at them, telling them they're not professional and if they want to play for your team, they need to change their attitude."

"That's very common," Vince said. "That's why it's so important to manage my state before the match or the practice session."

"Yes, managing your state is a key skill," Andrew admitted, "and what if you create an environment where it's even easier to do it?"

"How?" Now Andrew had Vince's full attention.

"Simply by telling your players, before you begin your talk, something like 'Today has been a very tough day for me. I don't want to give details, but if you see me more serious or less patient than usual, there's a reason and I excuse myself now if that happens. I'll do my best to keep my usual standard'."

"That would change my players' behaviors. They probably wouldn't joke around as much as they would have."

"Correct. And you probably would manage your state more easily. Can you see why disclosure improves your relationship with the team? You don't need to tell everybody about yourself and your problems—in fact you didn't—but just enough so that your players can understand your behavior."

"Now I see. In this way, I can help people around me better understand what they see and hear from me. This will expand my open area and the hidden area will become smaller." While saying this, Vince drew a line in the figure.

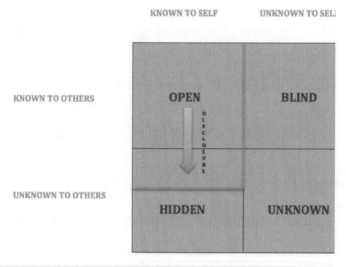

"Good guess," Andrew said smiling. "You're getting the point."

"And I'm sure you can also expand the open area on the other side, right?" Vince continued.

"Correct and you can do it with feedback. This is the most important tool ever. That's why I say 'the feedback culture.' The only chance you have to expand your open area on the right side is when you belong to a real team and you're surrounded by people who tell you what they think. In fact, when others say what they see (feedback), in a supportive and responsible way (and you are able to hear it), you begin to test the reality of who you are and you start growing. In this way you can do this," and Andrew drew another line.

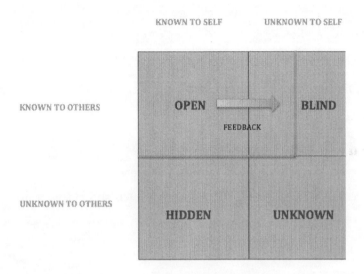

"But this requires a lot of courage, both for the ones who tell and for the ones who listen," Vince said.

"Actually, it's only a matter of culture. We know that every feedback is not about the person. It's about the behavior. We don't criticize people around us. We don't pass judgment. We only say what we see and hear. It's time to show you. Come with me and you'll understand what I mean."

Someone knocked on the office door. "Excuse me, Coach. Did you want to see me?" The team captain entered the room.

"Yes, please, come in Luke. This is Vince Longman."

"It's a pleasure to meet you," Luke said. "I'm a big supporter of your team. I've noticed that you've had a tough start, but you have a great team. I'm happy for you!"

"You're right and I'm here to learn how to make it even better." They all smiled. Then suddenly the atmosphere in the room changed. Vince started feeling uncomfortable, not knowing whether to stay.

"Yesterday, during the team meeting," Coach Hawk began, looking Luke in the eyes. His voice was confident but soft at the same time. "You didn't say a word until I asked you some questions. I felt like I was alone in a situation that we were supposed to manage together. Please, next time, tell your point of view, so we can be more effective as a team. We both want the team to succeed and I need your help with that."

"Okay. Thank you, Coach," Luke replied.

"No problem. See you on the court later." Coach Hawk shook Luke's hand.

"Bye, Vince. It has been a pleasure to meet you. Come see a game sometime."

"Yes, sure. See you," and then Luke disappeared. Vince was shocked. If he dared to say something like this to his team captain Herb Whiters he could end up in big trouble.

"I know what you're thinking. You think it won't work with your team, right?"

"Actually yes, I was thinking about some of my guys who wouldn't necessarily appreciate this kind of judgment—."

"That's the whole point!" Coach Hawk interrupted. "What you just saw is the end result of the feedback culture. First you need to instill it in your team. And you will understand that this thing is as far from any form of judgment as there is."

"Let's say I could do it. Is there a structure for good feedback?" Vince asked, looking for more information.

"Of course there is, and it's very simple." Andrew waited for Vince to take out his notebook again.

"First of all, good feedback always has four characteristics:

It's CONSTRUCTIVE: It doesn't degrade the other person, but simply points out the consequences of his behavior, action or choice.

It's EMPATHETIC: It's personal and subjective. It supports the person and expresses comprehension and cooperation.

It's NEUTRAL: It doesn't judge or interpret the reasons that led the person to act in that specific way, but it highlights facts, attitudes and behaviors that the other can eventually change.

It's CLEAR: It's detailed and easy to understand, and it provides suggestions or alternative behaviors."

Vince was taking notes furiously and the more he wrote, the more he liked the concept and wanted to know more about it.

"When you talk to the person, always have those four points in your mind and follow those simple steps:

Describe the situation: Be specific about the moment you are referring to.

Describe the behavior: Tell objectively what you saw, heard, touched. Not ideas, but objective facts.

Express how you felt or the consequences of his behavior: Tell your personal (or group) reaction.

Suggest appropriate alternatives: Tell him how you would like him to behave next time.

And when you're instilling this culture in your team, every person can answer in one of these four ways:

'Thank you!' – It means they got the message and it's fully understood.

'Tell me more, explain it better.' – They are looking for more information about the behaviors or the situation.

'Stop it! It's enough.' – If they got the same feedback from different people and they reach the point of 'enough is enough,' this is the perfect answer.

'Can you tell me if it happens again?' – They need more feedback about the same behavior and they accept coaching from teammates.

These four possible answers don't mean to limit the freedom of the other person, but are perfect to practice better listening, to avoid excuses or comments, to reduce chances of conflicts or unnecessary discussions."

"I'm beginning to understand now," Vince said. "That's exactly what you did with Luke! You started out describing the situation 'Yesterday during the team meeting...', then you described the behavior '...you didn't say a word until I asked you some questions...' and then how you felt '... I felt like I was alone in a situation that we were supposed to manage together...' and you finished with the suggestion '... Please, next time, tell your point of view so that we can be more effective as a team.'" Vince was excited at this point.

"Absolutely yes! And then I finished pointing out the common goal and direction: We both want the team to succeed," Andrew finished.

"I'm impressed! And I think I got your secret: The effectiveness of this method is that there is no judgment," Vince said. "What creates conflicts or raises barriers often is a judgment, for example, statements like 'You are insensitive,' 'You always put me in doubt,' 'You don't let me play my game,' 'You are too aggressive,' 'You wanted to punish me,' 'You don't trust me.'"

Coach Hawk smiled and nodded while Vince continued, "Judgments drive people to raise barriers and then they feel compelled to justify their behavior, even if they are stupid behaviors. Instead, if you express how you feel, most of the time the other person will accept what you say without fighting back." Andrew grinned proudly. "That's it exactly. In this case, you're simply sharing how a behavior made you feel and no one can say 'this is not true.' What you will often hear is something like 'It was not my intention' or 'I just wanted to...' and you can have a different interpretation of the situation and clarify what happened." "Wait a minute! If I work on both disclosure by telling my players and feedback by asking my players, I can improve and access a little bit of my unknown potential." while Vince spoke, he drew a circle on the figure.

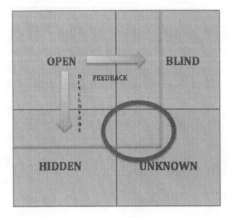

"Bingo!" Coach Hawk exclaimed.

The door opened again and this time it was Coach John coming to pick up the guest. "How did my kid behave?" John asked.

"Very well. He's a fast learner. I'm sure he'll do a great job!"

"Thank you for your time, Andrew. I really appreciate your kindness."

"No problem, Coach John. You know I will always be indebted to you. If you need anything just ask."

"I will," John smiled.

During the trip back to the stadium, Vince told Coach John all the information he had learned that morning. He was excited, like a child who had just opened his favorite present and was going to play with it as soon as he got home.

As usual, before going to bed Vince wrote in his notebook:

Notes to myself:

- ✓ *Use "Lombardi Time": Think and move fifteen minutes ahead.*

- ✓ *There is a moment for discussion, then the team has to make a decision and everybody needs to be aligned. Alignment means to behave in the way the team decided without necessarily agreeing with everything.*

- ✓ *There is no positive or negative feedback: Feedback is feedback. It's good to instill the feedback culture in the team, so everybody knows the importance of disclosure and feedback and can enlarge their open area.*

- ✓ *Great feedback doesn't judge the person. It's about the behavior and its consequences on me or the team.*

- ✓ *With disclosure and feedback you can access your unknown potential.*

HOW TO START A WAR

September 17

The next day, Vince woke up early with a mixture of excitement for the new strategies he had learned and with concern for the situations he wanted to resolve quickly. First on the list was Old Guy Tyler. Vince had to make sure that in the future Old Guy wouldn't behave like he did during the last game. When Vince arrived at the stadium, he ran into his office where Coach John was waiting for him.

"So what are you up to?" John asked.

"First of all, I asked Old Guy to come to my office so I can give him feedback about what happened during the game. I want him to play for the team, not for himself. I'll fulfill his need of significance so I can count on him from now on."

Someone knocked on the door and Vince opened it.

"Hi Steve," Vince began. "Thank you for coming without notice."

"No problem, Coach. Good morning, Coach John. How can I help you?" Old Guy asked with caution, looking at Coach John in the corner and then back to Vince.

"Actually we don't need help. Instead I'd like to talk about that ball you were supposed to pass to James during the last match," Vince said firmly.

"Coach, I know what you mean," Old Guy immediately replied, "but I had the field wide open and I knew I could score. It was only bad luck."

"Stop it! You don't have to justify your behavior. I'm here to tell you that you created a big difficulty for the team," Vince continued to be firm.

"Coach, excuse me, but I think the bigger difficulty is generated by certain people who don't commit enough during practice and who think everything is entirely due to them. And if you keep treating them like superstars, they won't learn how to work as a team," Old Guy answered, annoyed.

"How can you talk about other people's teamwork when you were thinking about yourself first?" Vince asked with the blood going into his head.

"Coach, if everybody thinks about themselves first, I'll do the same. At the end of the day, nobody cares how much you give to the team. Only numbers count. And my contract depends on how much I score. So if you want me to help others, I want others to help me, and this isn't happening now!" Old Guy was looking at Vince with resentment in his eyes.

Coach John was tempted to intervene, but he decided that this could be a great learning experience for Vince. He needed to understand the difference between applying a technique and knowing where you are going by calibrating what's happening moment by moment. Vince had just fallen into the big trap of judging the person instead of the behavior. Clearly, his goal was to be right rather than generating a different behavior that could convince Old Guy.

"Tyler, I don't want to discuss this further. This is a warning. Don't do it again or I'll have to take action. And you won't like it!" Vince yelled.

Old Guy, with a defiant look, kept his breath. "Okay, Coach. I understand. Is there anything else you need to tell me?"

"No, you can go!" Vince looked away.

"See you later." Old Guy slammed the door as he left.

Coach John looked at Vince. "So do you believe you convinced him about behaving differently?" he asked.

"Actually, no. I can't see the benefits of this Johari Window thing. He clearly didn't get it. And his aggressive way of responding . . . I'm not sure I'll use it again. It sounded so clear yesterday, but I'm not sure it works in a sports environment!"

"Well, before you quit so quickly maybe we should analyze the situation a bit. Did you give him feedback so he could enlarge his 'open area' and become a better team player? Or maybe you just threw your anger about the situation at him? Did you do it in order to help him or to vent? There's a big difference. Remember the golden rule: We don't judge or the other person will get defensive. You actually started out using the feedback model correctly, describing the situation, but you forgot one major component and that's one that I thought you knew."

"Oh yeah? Now what did I forget? I think what I forgot is what I was good at. Maybe I should go back to the league I was in before. I seemed to have a better grip of things." Vince sounded and look frustrated.

Coach John felt it was time to step in and stop Vince from becoming even more upset with himself.

"Listen Vince, you started out right, but you only forgot the basics in conflict management. That's all. I know you normally take this into consideration. Maybe it's unconscious behavior on your part, but as far as I know, you always go for the ball and not the man. But with Old Guy Tyler, you forgot and went for the man, so it became a matter of being right instead of just giving feedback".

Vince sighed. "You're right. I lost myself. That was stupid. I always focus on the ball and never go for the man, but today I forgot. I think I may be trying too hard to do everything right away."

"Well, nothing wrong in that," Coach John replied. "When you practice, you sometimes makes mistakes, but when you have too much on your mind at once, some things are forgotten. I don't know if you've heard about a guy named George A. Miller? He's a psychologist and he came up with the notion of 'The Magical Number Seven Plus or Minus Two'."

"Can't say that I have," Vince reflected.

"Well, the idea is that you can only handle seven plus or minus two pieces of information at the same time in your conscious mind. And that's on a good day! So with the pressure you're currently under, it's probably more realistic to say that you can handle two to three plus minus two right now. That's also why I only introduce one new topic to you a day."

Vince nodded as if he understood and John continued, "Normally, your well-established unconscious behaviors would be maintained – like going for the ball as you said you always do – but in this case, the conscious mind was using so much energy that you got carried away. It's my fault. I should have seen it coming, but never mind. Done is done, so the only question is what will you do about it now?"

Vince thought about the question and replied, "I should probably find Old Guy and apologize. I think that's the only decent thing to do."

Coach John nodded with a smile. "That sounds like a good plan, but before you do that, let's just quickly go over the steps of conflict management to make sure your brain remembers, because I'm sure it's in there." Coach John looked at Vince and waited for him to agree. When Vince acknowledged, John asked, "What's inside a conflict? What does it consist of?"

Vince thought about it for a moment and then said, "Whether we ourselves are involved in a disagreement or we stand outside it and try to help, the problem often seems endlessly confusing. There are so many elements, so many feelings and the big question is 'where to begin?'. My understanding is that there are four basic dimensions: The instrumental dimensions, the dimensions of interest, the dimensions of values and then the personal dimensions."

"That's correct," John said, "and what do they represent?"

"The instrumental dimensions are when we disagree about objectives and methods: what to do and how to do it. At this level, we just disagree and have to find a solution in order to get on with the matter. We must solve the problem. We have these types of conflicts very often; they seldom lead to problems and are often useful for creative decision-making. This is where I should have stayed this morning instead of allowing my personal feelings to take over. Then there are the dimensions of interest and they occur when there is a competition for resources that are sparse or appear to be sparse. The resources could be money, time, or space. Come to think of it, we could see contracts for the players or time on the field as sparse resources—thinking back to our conversation two days ago about Bob Fisher and his role on the team. At a larger scale, looking at the whole organization, it could be the fight for power and position in the hirearchy. In conflicts of interest, we have something between us where we cannot necessarily get everything that we want and, therefore, we may negotiate and find solutions." Vince talked with a solid and stable voice. Obviously, he knew all of this and yet he had forgotten this morning.

"So how can we solve conflicts in those first two dimensions?" John asked.

"Simple negotiation is all that's needed. People just need to percieve that what they are getting is a fair exchange for what they give up!" John nodded and Vince continued. "Dimensions of values appear in a conflict when values that are precious to us are at stake. These are the values we're willing to stand up for. It might be moral values. What is right and what is wrong? It might be values of our tradition, or of religion, political beliefs and dedication to human rights. And of course, because of the significance of these topics, the conflicts will now be more deeply rooted, which leads us into the personal dimension of conflicts, which often infects our personal existence and everyday life and creates vast confusion and suffering. Here, deep and sometimes hidden feelings play the leading role, and the parties become uncertain and vulnerable: Do others regard me as somebody? Does anybody see me at all? Can I trust them? Am I kept out? Do they despise me? Am I being respected? I believe I went very quickly to this dimension this morning with Old Guy, because it quickly became for both of us a matter of being right and respected . . . Not smart."

"And how do we solve conflicts at the last two levels?" John asked.

"By creating a mutual understanding", Vince said.

"Sounds like you have it all nailed down. So what's the catch?" Coach John asked with a curious expression on his face.

"Well, the catch is that in real life these dimensions are often completely entangled. When two players or coaches have a dispute about which play to play, it may look like an instrumental conflict. But it may also be a conflict of interest. I'll give you an example! Who has the right to decide? And maybe there is even a fight for power or esteem. Maybe it's even a personal conflict. Coaches and players have strong feelings and so may not be totally objective."

"But if it is true that the dimensions, in many cases, overlap one another, what is the purpose of distinguishing? What's the point of a model like this? Why spend time on analysis?" Coach John again asked the facilitating question that would bring the knowledge to the surface for Vince.

Vince responded, "Because in any conflict, one of the dimensions is always more significant than the others. We can call it the center of gravity. It's useful to sort out the threads from this basis. If there are deep emotional problems in one part or both, then these emotions have to be communicated in order to create a mutual understanding and acceptance of the other party's perspective. This isn't the same as agreeing, but rather accepting that the other person or party has the right to his or her perspective, and only after that can we expect the persons to act sensibly and stick to the point. Furthermore, if there are real and serious conflicts of interest between two parties, then these interests must be addressed, and the disagreement cannot be managed as a problem of emotions."

While explaining, Vince had drawn up the four dimensions on the flip chart, mostly as a reminder to himself, but also to show Coach John that he knew about this.

Almost as a reminder to himself, Vince repeated that in most conflicts there are more than one dimension involved and you need in most cases to establish a mutual understanding before negotiating solution…

1 - Instrumental dimension

About: Tangible issues like methods, procedures and structures.

Approach: Problem solving

Desired aim: Solution

2 - Dimension of interest

About: Allocation of resources like time, money, labour and space.

Approach: Negotiation

Desired aim: Agreement.

3 - Value dimensions

About: Political, religious & moral values

Approach: Dialogue

Desired aim: Mutual understanding

4 - Personal dimensions

About: Identity, self-worth, loyalty, rejection etc.

Approach: Dialogue

Desired aim: Mutual understanding

"Now, as I said, instrumental conflicts and conflicts of interests may be solved by negotiation. We can discuss how to do things and we can discuss what benefits to obtain. We can even reach agreements and solutions. But we cannot compromise our beliefs to come to an agreement and we cannot compromise our feelings. What we can do is have open communication and a dialogue about those feelings. If this dialogue occurs, the result may be that we reach a better understanding of the other person and of ourselves. That creates a friendlier atmosphere, which eases the negotiation of the opposing interests and instrumental points of view."

"Wow!" Coach John said. "You could teach this!"

"Well, actually I have," Vince replied. "And maybe that's why I got so frustrated when I goofed up this morning. I should have known not to do this and I should have handled it better!"

"Should have, could have, would have. It doesn't really matter now does it? The main thing is that you're willing to do something about it! So let's just quickly go over the next couple of steps in conflict management."

Vince nodded and continued, "No two conflicts are alike. They are all unique, no matter where they take place: in the individual, between two persons or among groups in an organization. However, conflicts can escalate in two distinct patterns. It's like a psychological code, some kind of script in accordance with which we act, when we let conflicts run away with us. These patterns appear to be somehow universal. It's good to know them. Being aware of them may lead to a certain reflection: Do we want to allow ourselves to just go along with the pattern? Or do we wish to act more independently and mindfully? Like

I said, normally, I always choose to break the patterns early on, but I keep kicking my own behind because I forgot this morning."

Vince, looking very annoyed with himself again, turned to the flipchart as if to prove to himself once more that he knew better. He made the following illustrations:

Visible conflict escalation

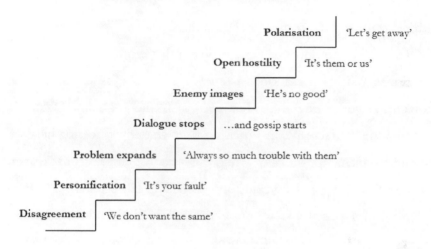

Then he turned back to Coach John and said, "There is the pattern of the visible conflict and it start with a disagreement. Nothing more, but just a plain simple disagreement. If we take a closer look at the visible escalation, we initially have a 'pure' conflict. The parties try to solve a problem that has arisen and to bridge their difference in opinion about how to think and act. At some point, one of them starts attacking the other, and the situation then escalates to the next stage."

John could see how Vince was twisting his face as he explained this part, because he was so much aware of how this was exactly what he had done himself this morning; he had allowed himself to become personal instead of keeping his eyes on the ball. John inserted, "The borderline between disagreement and personification is crucial. Once it has been crossed, emotions will flare and conflict will escalate. Usually one of the persons starts to reproach, threaten or offend, and the other person joins the quarrel. So the question becomes 'How can I respond mindfully to the aggression without yielding from my goals?' The further we ascend the conflict steps, the harder it gets!"

"Right," Vince said. "Now the problem this morning is that I made it personal. When I transitioned from addressing the issue that was the problem to addressing the other person as the problem, I actually escalated the conflict myself. When we both started expressing how we felt and we blamed it on each other, our negative emotions took over. We started blaming and attacking and defending ourselves. From there, the problem expands and we start to think of many other flaws and defects in the other party, other problems he or she creates. Suddenly, we remember unfinished business with the other. Old unresolved conflicts emerge, together with the recollection of old injustices and, by doing that, the tensions grow." Vince looked at John. "You know, it's amazing how fast this can happen. I mean, I spoke perhaps only a couple of minutes with Old Guy and yet we managed to get the conflict pretty high up the ladder!"

John nodded with a reflective look on his face and said, "The negative emotions blur our ability to think, and we communicate inaccurately. We don't speak clearly and we certainly are not able to listen attentively. We twist each other's words and we can't really hear what is being said. This is sometimes called 'the dialogue' of the deaf.

Conversation becomes too disagreeable, since obviously words are not sufficient, and we think 'Haven't I said so one hundred and one times?! It's no use!' We begin to avoid talking with each other, and instead we talk about each other, to others. We start to gossip in our concious or unconscious search for allies, and we form parties. Talking about each other, instead of with each other, is a clear indication of aggravation. Now, of course, it depends how you talk about the conflicts. Sometimes talking to an outsider about the conflict may make us more clear and ready to re-establish the lost contact."

Both men seemed eager to share this important knowledge and Vince took over and continued, "The more we narrow and close our mind about the other person, the more locked up and explosive the relationship becomes. The other party turns into a subject of projection. We see in the latter everything bad that we do not want to recognise in ourselves. At this point, the original disagreement has almost disappeared, and our goal is now to prove right, to triumph or even to harm the other. It is him or me, an eye for an eye. We are right; our goal at present is to prove right all the way. Only one reaction from the other party will suffice: Concession, apology, total surrender. We have become fundamentalists. Oh, I could kick myself! This is exactly where we ended up and I know I keep repeating myself here, but I just can't believe how fast it happened."

Coach John broke in, "The conflict can become like a magnet, like a black hole in the universe: It sucks in all light and energy, and we are so occupied with it that we can hardly speak of anything else. We hate it and, at the same time, we cannot stop thinking about it and this can lead us to open hostility, where we are no longer able to see the other person as a human being who, just like ourselves, basically wants peace and fairness, and who suffers by the conflict. Therefore, we escalate to open, hostile actions, bodily or verbally. The end justifies the means. We have seen people in this situation still trying to negotiate, and they claim they try to see the matter from both sides, but often without success. Harmful actions may now accelerate, from simple bullying to much worse things and that, of course, leads us to the point of polarization. At this point, the parties can no longer stay in the same place. This is the time of sackings, notices of resignation, flight, and establishing ghettos. One takes flight or is driven away. The best thing that can happen now is that the parties have no further contact. The worst thing is that they carry on with the war from a distance. But of course, there is always hope, since the possibility of reconciliation always exists in human hearts."

Vince looked at John and said, "However, if people do the opposite – if they withdraw or evade – can the conflict then develop, as well? Yes, it can! It is perfectly possible to escalate a conflict and avoid it at the same time! It's called an 'invisible conflict' and it basically starts the same way as a disagreement in which the issue and the person are still separate. We don't want the same thing, but all we have to do is solve the problem! However, for some reason I decide not to tell the other person, so he or she doesn't even know we have a conflict, which then leads to me making inner pictures. This stage is the test that will determine if the conflict will have a destructive outcome or not. From being just an 'issue', the problem expands and becomes personal. You start trying to interpret the other party's words and attitudes. You begin to fantasize and the whole thing goes on inside your head. You discuss and argue with yourself, doubt yourself and often end up concluding that it is the other person who is not right. From there, you begin to withdraw. Where you would have said 'yes' before, you now say 'no', but nothing about why you say no. The conflict is silently escalated without sending any significant signals to the other party. If the counterpart also withdraws and doesn't investigate what's going on, this person will also start to construct inner pictures. A sense of powerlessness may occur and other emotions may be involved. Now issue and person are also mixed for the other party. Now the conflict has grown so much on the inside that it becomes inevitable to talk out loud about it with others. This can go on for both parties. Gossip is very well-suited to strengthening the inner pictures we hold of others. It confirms our beliefs to share with others and helps us prove to ourselves that we are right. If the other person passes by, silence occurs. Each party stands on their rights and they regard each other as reprehensible! The conflict has now become an integrated part of behavior. Lots of energy is spent on controlling our own thoughts and reactions. In this stage, the 'room' is drained of energy. All energy stays inside each person. It becomes important to control the verbal communication and what brain and body is full of cannot be said!"

Vince, almost out of breath from his long lecture on invisible conflicts, turned to the flip chart and created the ladder for invisible conflict escalation.

Invisible conflict escalation

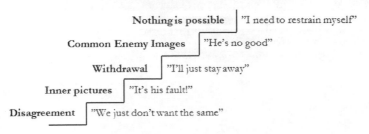

Nothing is possible — "I need to restrain myself"

Common Enemy Images — "He's no good"

Withdrawal — "I'll just stay away"

Inner pictures — "It's his fault!"

Disagreement — "We just don't want the same"

Vince turned back to John and laughed, "You know we could perform a show with this. It's like we both know. Can I ask you something? When was the last time you knew, but yet forgot in the heat of the moment?"

John thought about it for a moment. "Not too long ago. I think it happens all the time. It's just that for some, it happens more often and for some, even though it happens, you can't tell as easily because they tend to have more invisible conflicts. This has to do with the three ways people generally respond to conflicts which are Flight, when they evade, ignore, postpone, wait, or give in, or they can choose to Fight, which is where they attack, defend, threaten, blame, or use verbal or physical violence. Now, in the ideal world, they would always meet the conflict with an Opening. This is where they acknowledge the situation, dare to examine it, to check, ask and be clear. All three responses are common; we use all of them from time to time. But if flight or fight become rigid reactions of the individual, or of a group as a whole, change may be needed. There is a great difference between deliberately evading because it is the wisest thing to do in a certain situation, and automatically evading because it is a personal habit to submit or take the easiest way out. The same goes for the response of fighting." John continued, "The two classic reactions are to evade or attack, when the adrenaline prompts us to either run or hit. There can be good reasons for both reactions, but they do resemble each other in that they cut off any real contact with the adversary and with the problem at stake. They are not parts of a solution, but an escalation of the problem. Many people say that they are afraid of confrontations and that they are evasive. Others have the wrong idea that conflict resolution is about being nice and submissive. Many conflicts arise from being aggressive and not listening properly. However, it is just as likely that many conflicts arise when we do not express frankly what we really mean to say, and when we do not say where we draw the line. On the other hand, if we can meet a conflict openly then we can make out what is going on before letting the adrenaline take over, by asking open, curious questions in which we dare to examine the situation instead of judging it. In this way, we can open many of the conflicts we meet. To act in this way means to be willing to have contact with the person who is opposing us and to confront the problem that causes the offense. It takes some practice, because being open is not often what we have learned at school or at home."

Coach John stopped his speech for a moment and looked at Vince. "Have you heard about a guy called Marshal Rosenberg?" Vince shook his head and John continued, "Communicating is to have verbal or nonverbal interaction. It is to speak and to listen. There are ways of speaking and listening that block our channels to others and to ourselves, and there are ways that open. An opening communication can be learned and practiced. But it can never be a technical skill. It has to come from the heart; it has to be authentic. Otherwise it does not make a genuine opening. Marshal looked at the language types used in conflicts and was able to differentiate it into I-language and You-language. This is fundamental in understanding conflicts: We all have our own perception of our surroundings and ourselves. My perception is invisible to you. I alone know how my landscape looks and really only partially. If you define me, you are attacking my territory, and I will start defending myself. That makes a dispute escalate. When I draw a line, I defend myself and avoid an invasion of my territory. That can be very useful. But I am not making sure that you understand what I want. And I am not at all making sure that I understand what you want. If I want to achieve mutual understanding, I must explain what lies behind my frontiers. I must tell you about the territory behind my borders, about what is on my mind. What I feel and what I want. It's a bit like the Johari's Window. In the I-language, I speak for myself. I take responsibility for myself and stay on my side of the field. I tell you what is on my mind, what I see, feel and wish. When I approach your territory, I do so by asking respectfully what you have on your mind. I do not blame, interpret or diagnose you. I ask and I listen. The I-language is relaxing and opening because it does not attack the other person and because it opens up and clarifies. It is very simple and yet, for some, very difficult to put into practice. And again, this is not a moral must. It is a possibility that we can choose if we want openness."

"But—" Vince tried to interrupt, but John continued.

"Interrupting or listening Vince? Why do we interrupt? Probably to maintain and force through our own perception of reality and not let the other person's points of view prevail. But, however painful it may be to listen to the other person's story, it is still necessary if the conflict is to be eased. And how the mind expands when it happens! A lot of conflicts are based on assumptions and misunderstanding the other party's universe. Often we forget to ask the other person what he or she thinks. Luckily, the truth about what he or she thinks about us is almost always less threatening than in our own imagination!"

"I guess you're right. I forgot to see things from Old Guy Tyler's perspective and I didn't ask him about it either," Vince sighed.

John was on a roll, so he continued almost as if he hadn't heard Vince's last comment. "We can ignore or we can show interest. The conflict escalates when we treat the other person without respect. It is healing to anybody to be treated with respect and interest. Not just with the spoken word, but by the attitude, the body language and eye contact. And when we show interest, when we want to explore their territory, we can use leading or open questions. The open questions are inquiring and curious, whereas we already know the answers to the leading ones. They are a part of verbal combat. Quite often, it isn't even the questions themselves, but the tone of voice and, hence, the attitude that makes the question leading or open."

"Are you saying that I use leading questions?" Vince asked.

"No, not that I have noticed. I'm just making a point here about the importance of the whole package. That's all!"

Vince thought about it for a while and then, in a more quiet voice, he said, "Although I shouldn't have allowed my emotions to take control of me this morning, I still think that Old Guy should blame himself for the situation."

John looked at Vince and replied, "You can blame or express your own wishes. Blame is widely used as a form of communication, but the outcome is doubtful. It is often more useful to express what you wish or need than to blame somebody because you do not get it. Same thing with making generalizations or being concrete. In abstract language, we often use words like the general 'one' or 'ought to'. We grant rules and views to the other party and make the responsibility vaguely general. We use the words 'always' and 'never'. In concrete language, we stick to the actual issue." John looked at Vince and asked, "Do you know anybody who have been divorced?"

Vince nodded and looked puzzled by this question.

"Well," John continued, "have you noticed how many times people tend to keep talking about the past and who did what? Now, of course it can be useful to disentangle the facts of the past. But many times it is not about finding facts, but more about blaming the other party or person and dwelling on the past, and going on and on about it may escalate the conflict. It is much more useful and productive to talk more about the present and possible steps to take in the future!"

"Well, I sure wasn't going on about the past," Vince said. "I just used the Johari's Window, but forgot about the most important thing: Not to attack the other person."

"That's right," John said. "Attacking the person or the problem! The important thing is to distinguish simply between the act and the person who carries out the act. Distinguishing between 'wrongdoer' and 'wrong doing'. We are not able to change as long as we are being defined negatively and, as you saw, Old Guy Tyler is a good example of someone who only heard the blame and the attack, so he got very defensive and then the whole situation exploded."

John took a fresh flip chart and wrote up what he had just explained.

OPENING - I-Language

- ✓ Genuine regret and forgiving
- ✓ Expressing own concerns and need
- ✓ Showing real interest
- ✓ Explaining own facts
- ✓ Listening to the other's story
- ✓ Calming & reassuring
- ✓ (Future relations)
- ✓ Sticking to facts
- ✓ Being sincere
- ✓ Expressing one self
- ✓ Listening to the other
- ✓ Attacking the problem: What to do?
- ✓ Frank language

BLOCKING - You-Language

- ✓ Superficial excuse
- ✓ Blaming the other
- ✓ Neglecting the other
- ✓ Ignoring or opposing the other's facts
- ✓ Interrupting the other's story
- ✓ Threatening
- ✓ Exaggerating
- ✓ Generalizing
- ✓ Using sarcasm
- ✓ Defending one self,
- ✓ Attacking the other
- ✓ Attacking the other: Who to blame?
- ✓ Rude or evasive language

Vince, standing by the window, suddenly interrupted John, "Sorry, Coach! There's something I have to do right away if you'll excuse me!" and without hesitation he ran out of the office.

John walked over to the window to catch a glimpse of what had caught Vince's attention so quickly and he immediately saw Old Guy Tyler down in the parking lot. John saw Vince run over to Tyler and, even though he couldn't hear what the two men were talking about, he was very sure that whatever Vince had said had been right because, just a few minutes later, both men shook hands and smiled at each other. Coach John couldn't stop himself from landing a big smile on his own face. He was now certain that Vince would achieve and overcome the obstacles he was facing now and would be facing in the near future. Maybe it was time for John to also have a little chat with Orlando Jives... the way he was talking about the players, with sarcasm and distance... surely not the "I-language" way...

Coach John realized that Vince, in his eagerness to talk to Old Guy Tyler, had forgotten to make his usual notes, so he took a fresh piece of paper on the flip chart in Vince's office and wrote on it:

Notes to myself:

- ✓ *Keep your eye on the ball – do not make disagreements personal*
- ✓ *Check which and how many of the four dimensions are present in any given conflict*
- ✓ *Pay attention to both the visible and the invisible conflicts*
- ✓ *Gossip is usually a sign of conflict somewhere*
- ✓ *If conflicts escalate too far up the ladder, third-party mediation is recommended*
- ✓ *Meet conflicts with an open and curious mind*
- ✓ *Talk I-language*

Coach John

MOTIVATING SPEECHES

"So, how did he respond?" Coach John asked when Vince came back to the office.

"Well, he was very understanding of the whole situation and he accepted my apology. I stressed that I regretted the way I had communicated, but also that it didn't change the way I felt about his actions. I told him that my expectations of him as a senior player and as one of the team leaders are different then the expectations I have of some of the other guys and that I need to know I can rely on him showing leadership both on and off the field—otherwise I can't use him."

"Okay, and what did he say about that?"

"Well, funny enough, he said that he is, of course, very aware of his role, but that with all the changes, he'd become uncertain of how much he's still considered a leader. He said that before, with Coach Mac, he felt more like a leader because he could act more autonomous and since I took over, he had occasionally felt like I didn't trust him as much, because I was more into the details of running things! I asked him why he hadn't confronted me with this before, and he told me that he wasn't sure about who I really am and what I stand for, so he needed more time to assess me before he could. I told him that for me it was quite the opposite. Since I hadn't seen him stand up as the natural leader, I had purposefully been more on top of him than I normally would be with a team leader. I told him I needed to see demonstrated skills before I would delegate fully and that I had not seen him demonstrate his skills that clearly. We actually had a good laugh about it, because he said he felt that I hadn't given him the chance to demonstrate it, even though I felt I had. What a big misunderstanding and I guess it shows how quickly our assumptions can lead into the wrong direction, when we don't examine and investigate them! We have agreed to work together and for both of us to meet later today with the other team leaders to discuss team leadership and mutual expectations, because right now the team doesn't have enough leadership and sound decision-making when I'm not around. I should probably call a meeting with the coaching staff, too. I think it's time for me to start putting all of this into action and to align our efforts and stress the purpose of each function and the team, so that we are all on the same page. We've had a rocky start this season, but we've not lost the race!"

Coach John could sense the urgency in Vince's voice and acknowledged, "Sounds like you've got yourself a winning plan. Before you meet with the team and coaches, may I remind you that you have an important game coming up, so maybe we could combine two things here. I'd like to work with you on your motivational speech to the team leaders, the coaching staff and the whole team. You need to nail all of them and you have one chance with each group, so it has to be spot on. Are you okay with spending some time on that now, or do you have other important matters you need to take care of?"

"What could possibly be more important than motivating the people around you? What are we waiting for? Let's get going!" Vince picked up his notepad, ready to make notes and generate motivation.

"First of all," Coach John began, "being able to do a great motivational speech is a key factor when you coach an athlete or a team. You need to get your team ready for the battle. Your players need to be in the perfect mindset and motivated to do their best, giving 100 percent on the field at all times. Everybody must play their roles—as leaders, as members of your coaching staff, as replacements, as players on the field. You want to move their emotions. You want them to commit to the team at the highest level in every single moment of the game, especially when the adversities come. The basic goal for a motivational speech is to persuade people to take action – which kind of action depends on your desired outcome. What do you want or need from your team leaders? And what do you want from your coaching staff? And what do you want from the whole team? These are the first questions you want to ask yourself and find answers to. Decide what message you want to deliver before you plan your speech."

Vince kept taking notes. "Okay, got it: different goals for different people and roles, and think about it in advance!"

"Yes. When you're clear in your mind what you want, then you want to communicate it in the most effective way. Most coaches underestimate the speech. They think they can improvise while they're speaking. You can't imagine how many times I've heard coaches who were supposed to be making a motivational speech and they were lucky if their athletes didn't fall asleep. As you prepare tactically and physically for the match, you want to do the same thing with their minds and their hearts, especially in the pre-game."

"Are there some specific elements I need to address during a motivational speech?" Vince asked, becoming even more involved in the topic.

"Yes. Every situation is different, but there are some commonalities in all motivational speeches. First, it's useful to create a 'yes set.' Have you ever heard about that?" John asked.

"It's when you make some statements that the listeners can only agree with, isn't it?" Vince replied with interest.

"That's correct, and it's a very important step. Before leading people in the direction you want, you need to pace them. It unconsciously creates more credibility and your athletes will be more willing to follow you."

While John spoke, Vince took notes madly.

"You can use sentences like: 'You're sitting here in front of me tonight...', '15 minutes to our biggest challenge...', 'Great moments are born from great opportunities and that's what you have here tonight'..., 'This is the third match of the season. We lost one game and won two in a row...', 'We practiced almost every day since August...', and 'We have two players out today and three people who are going to play in a new position...' Actually, it doesn't matter what you say. You can speak about the current situation, the opponent, the press, or simply what they are seeing, hearing, smelling or touching. Just make sure to say something unquestionably true and you'll train their unconscious to say 'yes' to more important things that will follow."

"We're talking every day for almost a week now and we want to prepare the next game for the better," Vince said.

"Of course," John replied.

"I got you! That was the beginning of a yes set," Vince said laughing.

"Damn! You got me," John laughed. "You're learning quickly. Now, the second element is to anticipate the negative consequences that will happen if they keep doing the same behaviors—the unproductive ones, if that's the case. It creates an 'away-from leverage' that will motivate some members of your team. At this point, suggest your alternative as the perfect solution to the current situation and tell them the positive consequences. Talk about behaviors. This will motivate the rest of the team. So now everybody is ignited. When they feel bad not doing the new behaviors and they feel marvelously doing them, you've created a propulsion system that will propel them to reach their goal. Then attach these new behaviors to the beliefs and the values of your team and make them feel part of something more important. To do this, you can use stories, anecdotes and examples. Players often respond well to a story or a metaphor, rather than a long speech. They usually have short attention spans and are often distracted with their own performance anxiety. A well-timed story will help your athletes relate to what you are saying."

"Okay. I need to prepare it meticulously," Vince said with enthusiasm.

"Yes, and then there are some communication tips", John said and wrote on the flip chart:

✓ *Have a clear opening, mid-part and closing (call to action).*

✓ *Use simple words.*

✓ *Master your voice tone and body language.*

✓ *Make eye contact with everybody and make them feel engaged.*

✓ *Give players time to process what you're talking about with a pause after key statements.*

✓ *Repeat key points.*

And, above all, believe in what you're saying. It must come from your heart. You're speaking the emotional language and you want to move emotions. That's the key!" John concluded.

Vince's eyes were wide open, he was electrified. What a great lesson and what a great tool. Before he could say anything, Coach John took out a sheet of paper from his pad and he gave it to Vince. "This is one of the greatest sport motivational speeches. It comes from a movie and it's inspired from a real speech by a real coach. The movie is Any Given Sunday and I'm sure you know it. I want you to read this and notice all the passages we talked about. Then go on YouTube and watch the video over and over again. Analyze Al Pacino's voice and movements and let you brain learn. Of course, this is a movie, but there are a lot of things that can inspire you," Coach John said.

Vince looked at the piece of paper and there it was:

I don't know what to say really.

Three minutes,

to the biggest battle of our professional lives,

all comes down to today.

Now either,

we heal as a team,

or we're gonna crumble.

Inch by inch,

play by play,

till we're finished.

We're in hell right now, gentlemen.

Believe me.

And

we can stay here and get the shit kicked out of us.

Or

we can fight our way back ... into the light.

We can climb out of hell.

One inch, at a time.

Now, I can't do it for you.

I'm too old.

I look around, I see these young faces and I think,

I made every wrong choice a middle age man can make.

I pissed away all my money, believe it or not.

I chased off anyone who's ever loved me.

And lately, I can't even stand the face I see in the mirror.

You know, when you get old in life,

things get taken from you.

That's part of life.

But, you only learn that when you start losing stuff.

You find out life's this game of inches.

So is football.

Because in either game,

life or football,

the margin for error is so small.

I mean,

One half step too late or too early,

and you don't quite make it.

One half second too slow, too fast,

you don't quite catch it.

The inches we need are everywhere around us.

They're in ever break of the game.

Every minute, every second.

On this team, we fight for that inch.

On this team, we tear ourselves, and everyone else around us to pieces for that inch.

We claw with our finger nails for that inch!

Because we know,

when we add up all those inches,

that's gonna make the fucking difference between winning and losing!

Between living and dying!

I'll tell you this:

In any fight,

it's the guy who's willing to die

who's gonna win that inch.

And I know,

if I'm gonna have any life anymore,

it's because, I'm still willing to fight and die for that inch

Because that's what living is!

The six inches in front of your face!

Now I can't make you do it!

You gotta look at the guy next to you.

Look into his eyes!

Now I think

you're gonna see a guy who will go that inch with you.

You're gonna see a guy who will sacrifice himself for this team

because he knows when it comes down to it,

you're gonna do the same for him.

That's a team, gentlemen.

And, either we heal — now! — as a team!

Or we will die as individuals.

That's football guys.

That's all it is.

Now, what are you gonna do?

Vince read it over and over again, pointing out all the yes sets, the consequences and also the embedded commands, the presuppositions and all the other language patterns he could find, thanks to his previous studies of linguistics. Much of his inspiration came from a guy named Dr. Richard Bandler, who for the last four decades or more has been exploring how to use language to influence the unconscious mind and generate lasting change in people.

Then he played the video and started watching on YouTube all the related motivational speeches by the greatest coaches: Vince Lombardi, Herb Brooks, Herman Boone, Ken Carter, Don Haskins and tens of other inspiring people. He spent all evening having fun on the web skipping from Rocky to Braveheart and from Gladiator to Martin Luther King, just to get inspired.

Vince wrote down every useful idea. The more he wrote, the more thoughts came to mind. He was feeling so good. He got his goals clear in his mind and prepared his speeches for each group. His first speech would be to the assistant coaches. He needed them for the team to succeed.

Before turning the lights off, he read the speech from Any Given Sunday again and heard it inside his own head with Al Pacino's voice a couple of times and the he made as usual a few notes on things that he needed to remember:

Notes to myself:

- ✓ *Pay attention to assumptions: They can lead in the wrong direction when we do not examine and investigate them.*
- ✓ *Discuss team leadership and mutual expectations.*
- ✓ *Motivational speeches are a key factor: Mind and emotions have to be ready for the game the same as the body.*
- ✓ *Motivational speech persuades people to take a specific action: Set your outcome in advance.*
- ✓ *A "yes set" creates credibility and a solid basement for the speech and the "call to action."*
- ✓ *I need to speak from my heart and believe in what I'm saying.*
- ✓ *Make my players feel part of something higher and more important.*
- ✓ *Prepare the motivational speech knowing your players.*

Coach John

SOLVING CONFLICTS

September 19

For Vince, it had been a couple of busy days. Not only did he have a team to lead, but he had to spend a lot of energy implementing all the new learning. Maybe Coach John had sensed that, because he had told Vince to focus on the Thursday night game and get the team ready.

His team of trainers had pregame drills for each of the players and combination of players, so they had done many of the things that needed to be done. So for Vince, it was mostly about getting his assistant coaches into the right gear and that's why he had summoned them all for a meeting to discuss the strategy in detail and see if there was anything they had missed.

"Good morning guys. I would like us to remind ourselves why we are here before we start the meeting. I know that we're still getting used to each other and that I have different ways of doing things compared to Coach Mac and that most of you worked for him a long while. But Mac isn't here anymore and it's my responsibility to get this team as far as we possibly can. We've had a rocky start and the last game was not pretty, but we won and I've spent some time going over the processes of both the players and the coaching team in order for us to find areas where we can be more efficient. But as I said, I'd like to start by reminding each and every one of us why we are here."

Vince stopped talking and looked around the table at the faces of his assistant coaches. They looked in suspense at him. What on earth was coming? Even Dumbbell Jack looked more interested than he normally did.

"The purpose of the coaching team is to develop and nurture, with direction and support, a championship team that can go all the way to the final game, not only this year, but also in the future." Vince looked again at each of the coaches and was anxious to see how they responded. He had been working on this sentence now for more than a week and it felt good and right when he sounded it out. He could see all the heads nodding slowly, but in agreement with what he had just said, and it made him feel good inside. This was a crucial step for the rest of the meeting. It was time to put things into action and he needed to get his assistant coaches on his side in order to do what he now planned to do with the team.

"If we look at the season goal, we probably all agree that being in the final championship game is what we are looking at. We might even say that we have a goal before that of getting into the playoffs, because if we don't get there, we are not going to get to our ultimate goal. However, I would like us to focus on the short-term goal, which is the upcoming game. But I don't want us to focus on it as an ultimate goal, but more as starting point for how we would like to work for the rest of the season and many seasons to come. We saw in the last game how individuals were ready to sacrifice the team performance in order to look good themselves. This is not acceptable. This is a team and there is no I in the word team. We are all part of it and it is a part of us all. We just have different roles to fill in. That's it."

Again, Vince calibrated the responses he was getting from his staff and still they all looked at him and nodded their agreement, so Vince continued.

"Winning the game tomorrow is vital, so we could say that the short-term goal is winning the game, but that would not and should not please you or me or the team or anybody for that matter. If we don't look like a winning team, it doesn't matter, so the goal for tomorrow is to win the game with a winning mindset and to look like winners, from the moment we get here to the moment we go home. It's a home game and each and every one of us, coaches and players, will walk with pride and commitment in our faces and our bodies. We will talk with pride and commitment and we will let people know that we feel that pride and commitment. We will warm up with pride and commitment and we will play with pride and commitment, and if we encounter any difficulties, we will fight back with pride and commitment, both on and off the field. We focus on the behavior, not the result, and then the result will become the consequence of our behaviors!"

Vince had built up his voice for each time he said the words pride and commitment in order to make them stick in the minds of his coaching team. He could tell that each time he said it, they sat more and more straight in their chairs and when he finished, they all growled like animals as a gesture to him of having accepted what he had just said. He continued, "Doing just that and nothing but that will feel good for the individual, for the team, for the organization, for the fans and for everyone with a heart for this sport!"

Again, his coaches growled in return.

"I need to know that I can trust you guys to do what it takes and that you are willing to support me in the quest for glory built on pride and commitment. I need to know that you won't take no as an answer, but that you are willing to sacrifice to get there. And I don't mean small sacrifices. I'm talking about the biggest sacrifice anybody can make to a team. I'm talking about giving up the ego and doing what it takes for the team. Glory will come from what we do together, not from our individual agendas! Are you with me?"

Vince, now totally pumped up, held his breath. This was the ultimate moment. This was where it would happen or not. This was his entry into the big league for real and he knew it and could feel his pulse. Slowly, the message began to sink in with the coaching team and sincere and determined looks appeared on the faces of every coach on the team. Vince had succeeded and he knew now that he could make it happen.

"Gentlemen, I'm proud to be talking to you today because we have just agreed and made a pact, a commitment to excellence and long-term pride, based on what we do and how we do it. We have had our differences and some of you have most likely questioned my methods and my skills. I had to learn a few things and I still have to learn many more, but I am willing to learn and I feel good when I learn. As you all know, I have had the privilege to have Coach John around me for more than a week and he has introduced me to some people who all had something to offer. Now I could have been vain and pretended that there was nothing to be learned. I could have continued to do it my way, but I have not. With my position, I could have felt embarrassment by being taken back to school, but I didn't. I've been proud of learning and committed to building excellence and this is where I would like us to start this meeting. If we agree that the goal for tomorrow is to win the game with a winning mindset and to look like winners, then we need to focus on that, to put differences behind us and to find ways to create that winning mentality. So I'm going to ask each and every one of you to speak up if you don't want to find solutions. If you don't, then please share your perspective on where we are and what's missing in order to achieve our goal. Please, do put your ego behind and feel free to say anything that can help the team, including criticism of me."

Before starting the round robin, Vince explained the Johari's Window and asked the other coaches to use that model because, even though it would be tough for some, he would end up with loads of precious information. After the round, he said, "Okay, gentlemen. Now let's look at what things we have in common, the things that despite coming from different angles and despite having been said with different words, that we can all agree on!"

He turned to his flip chart where he had listed the main points from each coach and started drawing lines between the similarities. Very quickly, he was able to come up with a short list of things that they all could agree on:

✓ *Leadership not always clear.*

✓ *Getting stuck in negative situations.*

✓ *Not clear what preferred behaviors there should be on each position.*

✓ *Unclear decision making on and off the field.*

✓ *Rules not known by everyone.*

✓ *Mutual accountability not present.*

"Good job guys," Vince said. "Now let's look at the needs and the feelings behind this. What does it mean when we're in those situations?"

Dumbbell Jack was the first to offer his point of view. "Well, when there's no clear leadership, I get confused about what I have to do and I'm the type who'll then go ahead and do it my way just to make sure that at least something gets done!"

The rest of the coaching team nodded. This seemed familiar to most of them.

Tony Ambroyio, the defense specialist and always good for a humorous remark, was next to offer his point of view. "Well, guys, you know me. I'm the joker around here and I always try to make people laugh, but lately, I've found myself holding back on that. What I've noticed is a sense of fatality and it impacts me so that I feel bad and out of my usual energy. What I need is for us to be able to turn the negative situations into possibilities and it would help if we could laugh about our mistakes."

Vince thanked Tony for sharing. He agreed that there had been too much focus on the grave side of things and he took his share of the responsibility for that happening.

Next to say something was Mark Matters. He was the analyst on the team and normally the last to say anything, so obviously every one turned and listened with great attention when he spoke.

"From my perspective, I'm missing some guidelines as to what we want in each of the players. I'm talking about mindsets, values and beliefs and what behavior drivers we need on each position. When I don't have that clearly pointed out, I don't know what to look for, and then I feel frustrated. I'd like us to some distinct traits that we could calibrate each position against. That would also help me in giving guidelines to our scouts out there. If we want to build what you just talked about, then it is vital that we get the players with the right mindset from the start."

"I couldn't agree more," Vince said. "It's a very good point and one I thought was clear, but I'm so glad you're pointing this out! That brings another thing to my mind," Vince continued. "I thought it was clear how we make decisions on and off the field, but over the last two weeks it has become clear to me that it is not. I get very upset when I see people making decisions on their own when they're not supposed to. I need to be able to trust the players and you guys, for that matter, that we stick to agreements and we stick to the decision strategy we have."

The Sergeant, as everyone called him although his real name was Tim Shobowsky, cleared his throat and said in his usual deep, powerful voice, "I think we need to have a more clear rule set, a code of conduct if you will, or we could call it norms for how we behave. I have seen behavior on this team—all of us included—that I don't find acceptable and most certainly not in line with pride and commitment as you were talking about, Coach, and when I experience that, I get so mad! I know you guys think I'm rule-obsessed because of my military background, but ground rules give people a chance to know how to conduct themselves. It gives them a standard they can abide to and it gives us a chance to call it to their attention when they're not aligned with the code of conduct we desire. I need that in order to give them constructive feedback!"

"Very good point, Tim." Vince made notes of everything being said, not only actions but also feelings, and in particular the needs behind the feelings. This was the most constructive meeting he had attended in a long time. Vince looked over to the corner of the room where Coach John was sitting and rocking quietly on his chair. "Is there anything you'd like to share? You've been with me, and us now, for almost two weeks!"

"Well, my intention was not to say anything today. This is your meeting and I don't think I should influence on your decisions."

"Cut the crap," Dumbbell Jack said with an unusual smile on his face. "You've been influencing more than any of us in here can realize." He continued in a more grave tone, "It's no secret that you and I have had our disagreements in the past and I, for one, did not welcome seeing your face last week. However, I think Coach said something that made me think. Was it my pride or my vanity that led me to hold onto old grievances? I realized it was vanity. You were right back then when you fired me and, although it was an unpleasant experience, I learned from it and I could still learn from it, I realized when I just heard myself talking a moment ago. I still can revert from time to time and start doing things my way, even when my way is not aligned with the overall goal, but when that overall goal becomes foggy, I start acting. Probably, I should start asking more questions instead, but that's my impatience to get results. So speak up and share. You want this team to succeed just as much as everyone else in this room, don't you?!"

Dumbbell Jack got out of his chair and walked over to Coach John and extended his hand. John stood and shook Jack's hand, then the two embraced and hugged each other. There was complete silence in the room and nobody said a word for a while.

When Jack got back to his chair, Vince said with a smile on his face, "Well, with that minor difference behind us, I think we would all very much like to hear what you got."

Laughter broke out in the room as a sign a big relief. Nothing could stop them. John was touched by the moment and you could tell from listening to his voice when he said, "I think what is missing is a sense of mutual accountability. When you agree on something and then that thing is not done, nobody seems to care or take action. When people do something that is not okay or acceptable, who steps in? Well, of course, Vince does and some of you do, but it should be everyone in the whole organization, including coaching staff, players and other staff members. Winning is a mutual thing. It requires team effort and the whole organization becomes the team. When that happens, it generates an atmosphere of 'We want this' and then magic can happen."

"Thanks, John. As usual, gold nuggets coming from you and you are absolutely right." Vince continued his note taking. He looked up and said to the group, "So let's brainstorm for solutions. I don't want just one solution for each item up here, but many, so that we can choose and agree on the best one. Would you guys mind if we called in the infantry in the organization? I'm thinking admin and management, people like Orlando, Julian and, if you don't mind, Miss Hollie, who has a degree both in leadership and in communication! She has been very useful taking good care of Coach John and I think we could all benefit from having a different kind of background contributing to our brainstorm!"

No one objected to the idea and Vince called for a short break while he got hold of the various people and got them down to the sweat box, as the coaches meeting room was called. Twenty minutes later, the meeting reconvened with the addition Orlando Jives, the GM, Julian Swish, the Press Officer, and of course the always stunning Miss Hollie.

"Orlando, Julian and, of course, you Miss Hollie. Thank you for coming and joining us with such short notice. We're about to start brainstorming for solutions to some topics and we thought we needed a bit of fresh thinking in here to supplement our brains. We have shortlisted six items for which we need solutions and at this point, everything is possible, and we're not going to decide on anything before we have as many good suggestions as we possibly can get. Miss Hollie, please allow me to remind the boys that you are not here because of your stunning looks, but because you have a better and more theoretical background than the rest of us together."

Hollie laughed and replied, "I appreciate you openness. It's tough sometimes to just be looked upon as a dumb blonde, who is only here because of looks. But I picked a man's world on purpose, because I love sport, and I want to work in sport, and eventually to take over Orlando's chair or have a similar one someplace else."

The way she said it made no one in the room doubt her intentions and focus went back to Vince standing at the end of the table.

"Okay, topic number one. Establishing clear leadership that can inspire and motivate people and preferably can develop and nurture our talents. Any ideas on that one?"

Everyone was eager to contribute and many good suggestions came up on the flip chart. Some of them very elaborate and others more simple. Afterwards, Miss Hollie said, "You know I have an honors degree in leadership. I've studied all the known models and looked at research on which ones actually produce sustaining results. I think with the scope you have, or I guess I should say WE from now on, and if we look at one of the definitions of leadership which states that it is an influence process, it is working with people to accomplish their goals and the goals of the organization. If you agree with that definition, I suggest the model from Situational Leadership. It's a simple and easy applicable model and it has the advantage that it takes into consideration the level of competence a person has on a specific skill. It also has the advantage that almost the same approach can be used by the leader when he or she shifts the focus from the individual to the team, and although slightly different things are taken into consideration, it makes it easy for the leader in action to remember what to do. So that would be my suggestion!"

Vince wrote it on the flip chart along with the other suggestions and said, "So now that we have heard some suggestions and what makes each of them great, do we have any favorites yet? Please come up here and put your initials by the suggestions you like the best. Much to everyone's surprise, Hollie's suggestion was the only one that had everybody's name by it. Vince noted, "It looks like people want to hear more about your suggestion. Would you care to fill us in?"

Hollie got up and walked to the flip chart. "You know, if we look at a player, they are typically signed because they can play a certain position well. Yet sometimes we need to shift them around and teach them how to play a new position!"

She looked at the coaches who all nodded. They knew exactly what she was talking about and how it sometimes went smoothly and easily and how sometimes a player had to struggle with the transition.

"Okay, looks like you know exactly what I am talking about. Now, the reason is that people, as they learn, go through four distinct levels of development and each has its own characteristics. I won't go into details at this point, but basically as they progress, they have different needs for direction and support, and if the leader does not take this into consideration you may lose the player because the player gets frustrated. Same thing with one who has been on the team and in the same position for ages. If there are no new challenges, the player can become bored and then start performing less. In any case, if we don't give people what they need, we cannot get the best out of them. This means the leader has to learn how to diagnose in order to find out what development level the player has on this specific task, and then give the direction and support as needed. When an organization has this fully implemented, the beauty is that you can generate self-leadership and get players to come to you and ask for what they feel is missing. Cool isn't it?"

Hollie certainly had the attention of the group, so she continued, "Now with individuals, we look at the specific task or goal at hand, and we look at the competence and the commitment at which they perform the task, but with teams, it's slightly different. With teams, the task becomes how well they work together as a group on a task and then we adjust the direction and support we give the team accordingly. Both models are simple and easy to apply, which I think is one of the major advantages, because we live in a fast world where things has to happen right away and often without too much thinking done. It will require training for you and the team captains, but I think you'll find it worthwhile. Even with just my knowledge and training, I could easily give you enough to get us going and then after the season we could have formal training."

Vince looked at his staff and guests. "What do you think? Are you convinced? Shall we take a vote?"

All agreed that Situational Leadership sounded like what the team needed as a whole and also to support the growth and wellbeing of the individuals.

"That was easy and thank you so much, Hollie, for sharing this important information with us. Would you mind being in charge of finding more information so we can get going on this?"

"Absolutely not, Vince. I would love to. Actually one of my old friends from college works there, so I'll get right on it."

With that taken care of, Vince looked at the flip chart. "Next thing on the list is getting stuck in negative situations. How do we change that? Does anybody have a model or a tool to get back on track?"

"Well, I think we need to have more humor in the whole organization" Tony Ambroyio said. "I know you sometimes think I'm the clown around here, but I'm not a clown, but very meticulous about applying humor because the brain works better when there are smiles and laughing. It's a chemical reaction in the brain and we start to think better and more creatively. So as far as I can tell, we need to learn how to change negative situations into positive ones."

Many good suggestions, some more serious than others, were promoted, but Julian Swish was the guy who came up with the best solution when he said "Reframing" and nothing more. The room went quiet and Vince looked at Julian and asked him to elaborate.

"Well reframing is a simple technique and, just like with Situational Leadership, we need things that are simple, so that they are fast and easy to apply. With reframing, you take something that has a negative connotation and change it into a positive one, either by shifting the meaning or by shifting the place it happens. Let me give you an example! Let's say the players complain that it's raining on game day. Now, for most of them, that will be a negative. How do we change that? Easy! If we start off by shifting the meaning of the rain, we could say something like 'Well, isn't it great that it rains so we don't get dust in our eyes when we play?!' or we could take the rain to a place where it doesn't rain and there is lack of water and say, 'Think about playing on a field where it never rains and where there is a huge shortage of water and then imagine falling down on the ground and how much that hurts!' Again, here it should be said with a smile but done the right way, it cannot only make people laugh, but it can also help them gain a new perspective and find the light at the end of the tunnel."

"Definitely worth trying and sounds like it's easy to do with a little practice and indeed something that everybody can do," Vince said. "What do the rest of you think about that?"

Mark Matters, always the skeptical one in the group, said, "Isn't there a danger that people can feel insulted by rejecting their complaints?"

"There is and that's why you have to exaggerate it so much that it becomes almost like standup comedy, so that there is no doubt that you're reframing. Remember, the whole idea is to generate new and more positive chemicals in the brain because that will allow for different thinking. It doesn't happen the other way around!"

Mark seemed to get the point and nodded with a reflective smile. He had gotten an idea about how the scouts could turn a rejection into a more positive experience.

"Wow this is amazing," Vince said and continued, "We have an important game coming up tomorrow and I think we need to focus on that for the rest of the day and tomorrow. The remaining topics I think we should continue after the game, and for the ones regarding decision making, rules and mutual accountability, I think we should include the team captains, so that we have everyone involved in the process. As for the requirements for what preferred behaviors there should be on each position, I would like each of you assistant coaches to come up with a draft for the players and the positions you are responsible for, and then I would like us to have a new meeting on Sunday. I know it's your day off, but that also means that we can have the whole day without being interrupted, so that we can focus on this. I'm sure Orlando would be okay with us ending the day with a visit to the best restaurant in town and that includes your wives! Everyone's okay with this? Okay! Pride and commitment!"

"Pride and commitment!" the whole group yelled back and went off to do what they had to do.

Coach John was left behind in the room. He noticed that Vince had forgotten his beloved notebook and couldn't help himself to a sneak-peek into it to see what Vince had prepared. He had just run the perfect meeting, getting the group of trainers back into the team of trainers. The notebook said:

Notes to myself
- ✓ *Agree on disagreeing and desire to find solutions.*
- ✓ *Each tells the story the way they see it.*
- ✓ *Find common headlines.*
- ✓ *Elaborate on feelings and needs behind the headlines.*
- ✓ *Brainstorm for solutions, find many.*
- ✓ *Decide and agree on solution.*

IGNITING THE CHANGE

September 20

Vince woke up with a sense of achievement and jumped out of bed, eager to get started on today's program. He had summoned the entire coaching staff and administration to a meeting at 8 a.m. and he wanted to be there ahead of time. "Lombardi time," he heard himself saying and smiled because he recognized the voice inside his head as the one of Coach John.

He had spent all of last night thinking about the game plan, but also about the significant knowledge gained from yesterday's very productive meeting with his assistant coaches, including the valuable input from Julian Swish and, in particular, from Hollie. What an asset to the organization, he thought, as he recapped what she had said about leadership.

"Leadership is an influence process. It's working with people to accomplish their goals and the goals of the organization." Vince could still hear her voice saying the words.

Hollie sure was an amazing person and what he truly liked was the way her looks bluffed everyone. She would go very far and he was thinking about how he could utilize her knowledge more. He felt certain she had more to offer and, although a good assistant to Orlando Jives, she could easily become the internal consultant and trainer on leadership and communication. There were people other than Vince who needed that.

He forced his mind back to the game and today's program. Again, he heard a familiar voice inside his head, "If you keep doing the same, nothing will change."

"John, stop haunting me! I got the point!" He laughed out loud as he got in the car. Things would be different from now on and he was eager and ready to start the change.

****

Orlando Jives finished his coffee. He looked at his wife and his two sons and smiled. He was indeed a lucky man. Great family, great job and now also a head coach who was becoming what they hoped he would become.

He chuckled and his wife looked at him. "You seem in a particularly good mood today. That's a nice and welcome change. What causes you not to think you are gonna die later on during the game, as you usually do?"

"Well, honey, it may sound strange, but I have a really good feeling about the team's performance tonight and more than anything, our dear friend Vince Longman has started to step into his role as the Head Coach and that makes my life easier, a lot easier!"

"So what is it that he's done since you suddenly can breathe again?"

"Last night before I went to bed, I received a text message not inviting me, but telling me, to be present at a meeting at 8 a.m. with the rest of the admin and assistant coaches. Can't remember when that happened last. He also invited us to a brainstorming meeting yesterday and he really ran the meeting well. It appeared to me as if he's regaining the respect from the assistant coaches and they came up with some really good stuff. Still lots to do, but sure thing, it's going in the right direction!"

"Well, I'm happy for you, my dear, and I wish you a great game. The boys and I will be there to support you." She kissed him and off he went.

While driving to the clubhouse, he thought about yesterday's meeting and, in particular, what Miss Hollie had said. He knew she was smart, but he started asking himself if he had given her enough responsibilities. She sure could tackle more demanding tasks than picking up guests and coffee and hosting Mr. R whenever he showed up. He decided to give Mr. R a call, because it was his idea to hire Hollie, so obviously she shouldn't be given responsibilities that Mr. R disagreed with.

As soon as Orlando hit the highway, he turned the radio off and switched to his hands-free set. "Mr. Ridgeback, it's Orlando. Sorry to call you so early. Do you have a minute? I just want to brief you on the latest events and I have a question for you."

****

Joe Ridgeback smiled when he hung up the phone. Finally things were falling into place. What a great day and it was not even 7 a.m. The call from Orlando Jives had been unexpected but welcome, and it told him that not only was Vince Longman beginning to improve, but so was the thinking in the rest of the organization. He had not told Orlando that he also was summoned for the 8 a.m. meeting. He would keep that as a nice surprise for everyone, but how gutsy of a young Head Coach to call in the cavalry like this, including the owner. He stepped into his limousine and greeted the driver with his usual smile. Great guy, never said much, but always knew what to do. If all people would only know what to do when, wouldn't life be easy?

He decided it was time to make an important call and, although still early, he wanted to catch up with Coach John before the meeting.

"Coach, good morning! It's Joe Ridgeback. Do you have a minute? Good! I just wanted to tell you that I think our little experiment is really moving forward now." Mr. R briefed John about the summoning, as well as on the call he just had from Orlando Jives and how that had warmed his heart to feel that Orlando was getting back into the game. For a while, Orlando seemed to have given up, but now there was hope.

"Anyway, I would like to ask you for a piece of advice. It is rather unusual, to say the least, that an owner is summoned in the way Vince has summoned me and everyone else, so I guess he has something very important on his mind. But I'm a little unsure of how I should act. It's his meeting, but at the same time I guess I'm expected to do something, say something, but have no clue about the reason for this meeting. To be honest, it's only my curiosity that allows me to be on my way without calling him first and asking him what the …. he is doing, but I feel he has a plan and on a game day, I don't interfere with a Head Coach's plan."

Joe listened to John's advice.

"Thanks, John. I really am so happy that you accepted this challenge. I do have one more question for you and this requires your utmost confidence. I know I shouldn't ask you, but I have to, because it is crucial that this remains a secret. Can I trust you with something that you cannot share with anybody else?"

When Coach John acknowledged, Joe pulled up the window between him and the driver and thanked British Ingenuity for this device that made his compartment soundproof.

"Well, I've not been totally open with you and for a good reason. What I'm about to tell you now is only known by me and my lawyer, who is the trustee for the family foundation. It's a family secret and we'd like to keep it that way, but I trust you and I need advice from someone from the outside. You're the only one I would trust this secret."

****

John was listening attentively to every word Joe Ridgeback said, and he was amazed that Joe trusted him so much, but also very flattered. When Joe stopped talking, John thought for a while before answering.

"I think you're doing an amazing thing here. Your heart sure is in the right place. I do understand your dilemma and you have my word that I'll never tell anyone. Regarding your question, my advice would be to go along with Orlando's idea. Vince suggested something along those lines as well yesterday and besides I don't think you're utilizing the potential as much as you could and should. However, there's a big difference between potential and skills, theory and practice. So what I would do is go along with the idea, monitor it closely and make sure that the needed direction and support are given. The answer to your second question, would I mentor? The answer is yes, I would be honored. If I may say so, I think at some point you should tell her! I'll see you at the meeting."

John had to stop the conversation as he had arrived at the clubhouse. He parked the car and got out. It was a perfect morning – crisp air, sunshine. It would warm up and would probably be perfect temperature by game time. But he didn't think so much about the game, but rather about what Vince was up to, as well as the information Mr. R had just given him.

*****

Hollie was excited. The way she had been included in the meeting yesterday and finally had been asked to share her knowledge. She didn't want to let her impatience carry her away, but sometimes it had felt a little annoying not being asked. She could feel that change was in the air as she parked her car outside the clubhouse and being summoned to this meeting told her that it was a good change, at least for her.

It was weird the way she had gotten the job in the first place. She had placed top of her class and earned two degrees in the time it normally takes to complete one. She had always been lucky to get some really good scholarships that had allowed her to get into the most prestigious schools and she had worked hard to get the best results. In a way, it was strange that she had gotten so much funding, but schools responded to good results and hard work and she, for one, would not complain about that.

At her graduation, she had intended to take a sabbatical and then consider a PhD in Leadership, but her dean had asked if she would like a chance to work with a really interesting organization. A friend of his had asked him if he had the right person for a Personal Assistant to the GM and Owner of a sports organization and, though it didn't quite fit into her plans, she had sensed that it could be a rare opportunity, one she shouldn't miss. So she gladly accepted and had now spent a little more than a year in this organization, learning and picking up coffee, but the real big challenges had not yet appeared and she had started to wonder if she should look for a different sports organization. She liked the environment, the focus on achievement and the buzz on game days during the season. She knew there was a lot to learn, but she also knew that she could handle a job like that. She just needed to get some more responsibility.

Normally on game day, she would spend a lot of time working on her looks. She knew that there would be cameras and reporters and that everyone should look their very best, but today she had decided that she would change her appearance to a more business-like look. So in her business suit and hair neatly, but tightly arranged, she stepped out and felt good and ready to contribute.

*****

Herb Withers did not feel at ease. It was quite normal for the Team Captains to have a meeting with the coaching staff on game day, but meeting at 8 a.m. when it was an evening game, that was unusual, and he wasn't sure he liked the idea. He had his pre-game rituals and, for an evening game, that sure didn't include getting up at this time of the day.

In the clubhouse, he bumped into Bob Fisher and Old Guy Tyler, who by the look of their faces were equally puzzled by this early meeting and the purpose of it.

"What do you think Coach has on his mind?" he asked the two other captains. "I sure don't like getting up at this time, when I have to perform in the evening."

The two others mumbled in agreement, but the meeting was about to start, so they didn't have time to talk. They grabbed energy drinks from the bar and entered the meeting room.

If they had felt uneasy outside, it was nothing compared to their feelings when they saw Mr. Ridgeback, Orlando Jives, Miss Hollie, and Julian Swish in the room, along with the rest of the coaching staff. What in the world was going on? Without their normal self-confidence and funny remarks, they sat down and nodded their greetings to the rest of the room.

*****

"Well, it looks like everyone is here, so we can start. Good morning to you all and thanks for showing up so early." The last remark was directed towards Herb, Bob and Tyler. "I would also like to welcome our very special guest Mr. Ridgeback, whom I invited to this meeting so that he could share his thoughts and hear mine. I know that for a pre-game meeting, it is rather unusual to have guests who are not coaches and players but I want to share something with you all and I need you all to be present when I do that!"

Vince looked at everyone in the room and he was careful to look them all in the eyes. He could tell there was suspense. He could tell they were curious. He could tell he had their attention.

"If we keep doing things the same way, nothing will change." He purposefully avoided looking at Coach John, but could sense his smile as John recognized his own words. "Today marks the beginning of a new era for this team. Today, we will change things and we will keep changing as much as we need, but never more than we can follow. Today is where we draw a line and don't look back. Today is where we put ourselves in the driver's seat of this bus. Today is when we decide to show what we've really got. The difference between champs and chumps is only one letter. Today, we focus on the 'a' and not the 'u' and from today forward we act as a team and when I say team, I don't refer to players only. I don't refer to coaches and players only. No, I refer to all of us, because we all want this, don't we?"

Vince paused for a moment. His last remark, although positioned as a question had had the command tone down at the end and came out more as a command and there was nothing else to do for everyone in the room but nod in agreement.

"I've summoned you all here because I need us to come to some agreements. I need us all to make a pact, but before we do that, I'd like to remind you all why we're here. We're here because we want to develop and nurture a team with an organization around it that – with the right kind of leadership – can generate a championship team that can go all the way to the final game, not just this year, but also in the future. Do you agree?"

Again, Vince looked around the table and saw everyone nodding their acceptance. So far so good, he thought to himself.

"We have much to learn and we cannot learn and implement everything tonight, but we can decide with what mindset we enter the field. We can decide with what attitude we play the game. Performance is a reflection of attitude and it's your time to decide what will be yours. I came in here today with the Pride and the Commitment to make this team the best team ever! Now I don't know what you were thinking coming here, but if you come on the field or on the sidelines today, I want you to be there with Pride and Commitment. Nothing more, nothing less!"

Vince could tell he had the full attention of the whole room. His strategy was working, so he went on. "As I said, if we keep doing things the same way, nothing will change. For that reason, I've decided to make some changes to the game plan. They may seem odd at first, but I'd like to explain it to you and have you acceptance before we leave this room."

Vince looked at Herb, Bob and Tyler. "In any game, there are two teams and if they play to win, they prepare. Some more than others, but they prepare. I have looked at movies of this team's games from the last four seasons and we have pretty much opened the games in the same way and then we've fought our way back, very often impressing people with our stamina and ability to come back. My question is why do we want to get behind before we go ahead? Simple question, isn't it? Well, yes, to a degree!" Vince answered his own question, because it really wasn't a question, but again more of a statement.

"We can do things smarter, but not if we keep doing them the same way. That's why I've decided to do something that you would normally not see at this level in the sport. We'll open in a way that our opponent cannot foresee. Yes, it involves a risk, but it's a calculated risk and it's worth taking. I need your full support before, during and after." Then he looked straight at Herb, Bob and Tyler. "I need you three to think team and to remember that there is no 'I' in the word 'team'! Tyler, you're our starting man and, Bob, you're our experienced back-up for Tyler, right?" They both nodded. "Right, and why do we do that? Well, we play like everyone else, with a fixed starter who opens the games the same way. I want us to shake things up a little bit. This time, I'll start Bob. This is not, and I repeat not, disrespect to you, Tyler. On the contrary. But I want us to come out with a different routine, one they haven't figured out. Bob, I won't keep you in for long, but long enough that they start calibrating to your playing style. As soon as we see them do that, I'll put Tyler in there. Tyler, you're the number one man and, Bob, you're the number two. We all know that but, Bob, I have a special request for you tonight. I know you already take good care of Hack Hampor and keep him in the game mentally, but tonight I want you to focus even more on keeping him sharp. When – and I don't say if – we get a big enough lead, I want Hack to get his feet wet in an important game. So far, we've only played him when we needed to. Today, we'll use him because we want to. Bob, Hack is still young and I know that many years ago you were young too." He paused and the room filled with laughter and the tense atmosphere softened. "Hack needs direction and support. He needs leadership and I want you to lead him when he's not on the field. However, in the opening phase, I want you, Tyler, to take that role with Hack until I send you on the field. Are you willing to support me on this one, no matter what happens?"

It was a tough one, particularly for Tyler, but they all nodded. Vince looked at the rest of the room, not surprised to see doubt in some of the faces. "I've asked you all to be present at this meeting, because a decision like the one I just communicated will be scrutinized by the press and by a lot of other so-called experts who all think they can do our jobs better. You will be asked questions about the wisdom of this move. I need to know that I have your backing, that you're with me and that we're A team that is in this together!" The way he stressed the letter "A" before team made his message very clear and Vince again looked into the eyes of each and every one in order to get their acceptance of his bold move.

"I have one more thing to ask." This time Vince looked at Mr. R, Orlando, Coach John, Hollie and Julian. "I know on game days you are normally up in the owner's booth. Tonight, I would be honored if you would join me on the sidelines as a tribute to the team and as a clear signal that we're one team. I want you to help the team win, whether it takes filling water bottles or cutting oranges or whatever. Will you do that for me and for the team?"

Alessandro Mora & Anders Piper

SECRETS AND SURPRISES

September 20

After the meeting, Vince sent the players to rest and then had the usual meeting with the assistant coaching team. John decided not to interfere. Vince was a man with a mission who had chosen to do certain things and now he had to concentrate on that.

John accepted an invitation from Joe Ridgeback to join him and Orlando for an important meeting. John had a very good idea what that meeting would be about and he rather looked forward to it. It was important and would also mark a beginning of something new. In the executive office, reserved for Mr. R, they all sat down and when Miss Hollie entered with coffee, Joe asked her to stay.

"Hollie, we've asked you to stay as we want to discuss your role in the organization with you!"

Hollie shifted a little bit and looked unsure of what to expect. Joe sensed that right away.

"Ha, ha! Don't worry. I think you'll find it very interesting and I hope you'll like what we want to talk about." Hollie eased into her chair and Joe continued, "You've been with us for more than a year now and, to be quite frank, we probably could have utilized your potential a little better. Coach talking about that today marks the start of a new era and we would like you to take a bigger part in that."

Joe paused and looked at John who returned his gaze and made a discreet gesture encouraging Joe to go on.

"What I'm about to say to you may come as a surprise, but hopefully you will see that it's to your benefit in the end." He paused again and took a deep breath. "To be honest, I'm a bit uncomfortable sitting here right now. But there's something I want to share with you. You may have wondered why we hired you in the first place, why there was no job interview and we hired you based simply on a recommendation from your dean."

Joe looked at Hollie and when she confirmed, he continued, "Well, my father was a great man and one who really cared about other people. He was also a modest man – one you couldn't tell had all the money he possessed. One day, his car was stolen outside a remote gasoline station and this was, of course, way before we all had cell phones with us all the time. He got a lift from a young woman who had her baby in the back seat. As they were both heading for the same place, they had time to talk while they drove. The woman was a single mom whose husband unfortunately died abroad in the service of the nation and now she was alone and had to work hard to make ends meet. The woman was determined to raise her daughter to a better life and brought the child with her from job to job, working several shifts a day in order to make enough to save for her daughter's eventual education."

Again, Joe paused.

"Well, my father liked this young woman a lot. In fact, he was probably attracted to her, but his own wife had just died a few months earlier, so he was not ready to meet other women. When my dad offered money to pay for his part of the gasoline, the woman, although poor, refused. This woman was way too proud to receive anything out of charity. Now, had she known who my father really was, she may have thought differently, but she just replied, 'Mister, you look like you need all your spare change yourself and I, for one, know what that's like. If you want to give money, find someone who needs it and make their day! I don't have much money and the money I have I save for my daughter to get a real chance in life, but I want to be able to look her in the eyes and know that I was able to give her just that.' When they got to their mutual destination, my father got out of the car and thanked the lady for her kindness. She continued on her way and he never saw her again!"

"Why are you telling me this?" Hollie asked, but her voice revealed that she was more on the inside of herself than outside. So much in the story could have been her mom's story.

"Well, my father recognized the pride in this woman. He didn't want to offend her in any way, so as the lady took off in her car, he wrote down her license plate number and as soon as he got back to his office, he got his people to track the car and find out more about the owner. He then instructed his lawyers to create a secret fund that could, in some peculiar and coincidental way, channel the funds to one particular person. Now, I didn't know about this until my father died and his most trusted lawyer told me. I then started investigating a little bit and found out that my father had made a very good investment.

The woman was gone, working too hard for too many years, but the daughter was doing more than well. In fact, she was about to graduate with honors from one of the most prestigious universities in the country."

Again, he paused and looked at Hollie, whose face was now as white as a sheet, with reality striking her hard.

"The agreement was never to tell you that you're the daughter of that particular woman, but someone believes it would be better for you to know and make some choices before you find out by accident anyway!" Joe paused again and looked at John, who returned his gaze and then looked with warmness at Hollie.

"Do you need a break here?" Joe asked, but Hollie shook her head.

"No please go on. I'm a bit shocked, but also curious to learn more."

"Well, really there isn't that much more. Thanks to my father, you got a slightly better education than your mom's money could have provided, but your results primarily come from your own attitude and hard labor and all of that is your mom's doing and influence. You would have made it anyway, but when I found out that you existed and that you were doing so well, it was easy to conclude that we should try to hire you. However, your skills go far beyond those of bringing coffee for me and Orlando. Orlando and John told me how well you came across with your skills yesterday at the meeting and they also told me that the way you presented it proved that you could be a great internal trainer. We have a huge staff at many levels and we need to improve the leadership and communication skills around here. And I'm not only talking about the administrative and event staff. I also think we should add theoretical knowledge to our team captains and coaches, in particular. I think I can make this short. Are you willing to take on this responsibility? We'll make sure you get sufficient training and whatever else you need. You'll have my continued full backing."

Hollie sat for a while, absorbing the news. In a way, she was angry. Why hadn't anybody told her before? On the other hand, she also felt embarrassed about having received funds for a different reason than she had thought.

"Well, this sure is a day for big changes, isn't it?" Hollie said and mastered a smile. "I would love to take on the challenge, but if I find that you treat or evaluate me any differently than anybody else in the organization, I'll leave immediately. I also need a guarantee that this conversation will never leave this room. I'm very grateful for what you and your father have done for me. Don't misunderstand me. But I'm now a grown woman. I have personal pride in what I do and I want to be evaluated for what I do, not for who I am or for any other irrelevant thing. Is that a fair request?"

"Hollie, it's more than fair. You know, I feel relieved having told you, but probably would have kept it a secret if it wasn't for Coach John. He really comes up with some good advice. I want to share one more thing with you!" Joe looked at Hollie, who now looked like she had had enough secrets delivered for one day. "Don't worry! It is nothing like what I just told you," Joe said with a warm smile. "I just wanted to tell you that the suggestion of making you our in-house trainer came from Orlando and John. Neither of them knew that the other person was suggesting this and neither knew your story when they did. They recommended the solution because it was the right thing to do."

Hollie looked over to Coach John and Orlando. "Thank you so much. That really, really, really means a lot to me. I cannot tell you how much." She had tears in her eyes, but not tears of sadness, rather tears of pride and joy.

*****

It had indeed been a busy and emotional day for a lot of people. The Team Captains Herb, Bob and Tyler had a meeting after the news from Vince in the morning and had decided that they would support the Coach in his decision. They talked about how they should tackle the team and the reactions there would be when the team learned about the changes in the game plan. They had arranged lunch with James Larson even though he was not a captain. James was the ultimate prima donna, who could make a big fuss about things if they didn't go his way, but with his charisma and energy, he could also be the ambassador they needed to convince some of the more skeptical players.

Initially, James had not liked the idea. He was the favorite target for Tyler and not so much for Bob, but Herb was the guy who finally convinced him when he told him about the extra focus on the team and the team stars there would be from media. So once James was on the team, it was just a matter of waiting for game time.

*****

The locker room was crowded. You could tell this group of men was ready to combat the enemy. The room smelled of testosterone and adrenaline. It seemed more crowded than usual, because extra visitors, including Hollie, were there, so the usual sexist remarks were just something that had to be taken lightly. Much to everyone's surprise, it was Hollie who first got up in front of the team.

"I know most of you guys think of me as a dumb blonde with a good body and that you're all my favorite bed partner. Well, tonight you can prove that, each and every one of you. I am not talking about taking you all to bed." She paused and waited for all the funny remarks to wear out. "No, I'm talking about something far more important. I'm talking about my heart, my heart for the game, my heart for the team and my heart for the organization. Each one of you can take a piece of that heart with you to bed tonight if you show me what you're really made of. I want to see leadership, not only in the Team Captains but also in each and every one of you players. I'm young, I'm inexperienced in many things, but today I've been given a challenge and I'm willing to take it. Tonight, you guys will have a challenge and you can take it and make it. I'm a woman in a group of men. Show me that you're real men, not from the dirty words you can throw at me, but from the actions you take on the field tonight. If you want that piece of my heart, you've got to show me Pride and Commitment. Who's ready to do that?"

At first, the entire room was dead silent. Then James Larson started growling like a madman hunting enemies. That started a growling that could be heard around the whole locker room section. Hollie had shown them the attitude that reflects performance and through her good looks and their locker room dialogue, they had recognized the will to win, the will to succeed.

Coach John, standing in the corner with Joe Ridgeback and the rest of the assistant coaches, smiled. This was going to be one hell of a night and if the team could keep up the spirit, it looked bad for their opponent.

*****

"Gentlemen," Vince began in a central position so that he could see each and every one. "If I can have your attention please!" Again, it was James Larson who hushed his fellow teammates. Vince started talking, at first in a slow and soft voice, but it quickly built up. "You train yourself hard and practice hard every day for hours… for what? So you don't lose? So you don't look bad? You get into the locker room, you change your clothes and get on the field every day for practicing schemes and tactics so that you're ready for the big events. You do this under the pouring rain and under the hottest sun. And for what? So that you hope things go well during the match?" Vince paused for some seconds looking for players' reactions.

"Every week, millions of people watch you and they project their desire of success that maybe they'll never realize, but that they dream of wildly. You're a minority of individuals who earned the privilege to become what most people want at least once in a lifetime: to become a professional player. Do you know that only about one out of every 50,000 players becomes a pro? This team isn't made of normal people.

It's made of extraordinary people who overcame a very hard selection. I don't believe you do everything you do just to go out on the field and hope to win, or try not to look bad. I believe that inside every one of you, there is a fighter's heart beating. A warrior who has already overcome strenuous fights, with determination pride and commitment, and who wants to show who he really is, and what he can do!"

The perception of time changed. Vince could have spoken for an hour. All the players looked hypnotized. Vince knew in that very moment that he could plant a seed in their mind, a seed that could grow and bring them to the next level.

"Honor all the efforts you've made to be here today. Honor the privilege of competing against yourself every week. Honor the team you are part of. Honor your teammates and, above all, honor yourself. The only thing that is given to you today is getting on the field with a winning attitude, no matter who your opponent will be. We play with Pride and Commitment! We play to win, not to not lose!"

That was it, Vince knew it. He needed only to close and call to action.

"As one of the best coaches ever once said, great moments are born from great opportunity. And that's what you have here tonight, gentlemen. That's what you've earned here tonight. Now go out there and grab the opportunity!"

Alessandro Mora & Anders Piper

IN THE WAKE OF THE GAME

Vince was soaked in his own sweat, but he was a happy man. So much of what they had worked toward over the last couple of weeks had come into action and carried them through a difficult game. He stood in the middle of the locker room and the players gathered around him.

"Gentlemen, I'm proud of you! We played one hell of a game, it was a hard game and we took some bad hits but in the end, we showed them all that we are on the right track!"

The game most certainly had been hard and not without cost for Vince and his team. The shock effect of their bold move had thrown their opponent off. They had taken an early lead and things looked great. As planned, they then shifted Old Guy Tyler in instead of Bob Fisher, again resulting in a score, but in that very first drive, Tyler pulled a hamstring. He had needed to run the ball himself in order to score and that had put Hack in the game earlier than planned. Hack played a great game and gained much respect, but now Vince was faced with the challenge of having only two quarterbacks and his main man out for a couple of games.

Vince looked at Tyler. "I could talk about a lot of individual performances, but we're a team so I won't, except for one.....Tyler, you made me proud. The way you took the lead on the sidelines before going in, and in particular after your injury, was impressive. To me, that's true leadership. It's not about you. It's about what you can do for the team. That's exactly what I was talking about before the game."

Looking at everyone, Vince continued, "We've come a long way these past weeks and we still have a long windy road ahead of us. We're not done with the hard work. We have only just begun. We still have to improve and we still have things we need and want to change. Today we surprised them, but they'll be prepared the next time. We need to look at some changes in how we play and in how each and every one of you thinks about the way you play. But for now, you all deserve to celebrate tonight. Team Captains, see you at the press conference."

The players all roared and Vince headed for the Head Coach office. His team of assistant coaches and Coach John went along with him. They were joined by Mr. R, Orlando Jives and Hollie.

"Great game, Coach!" Mr. R was truly happy and excited. In the back, Orlando nodded his approval as well. "And thanks for having us on the sidelines today, it made it very special, I hope we weren't in your way at any time."

Vince looked at Coach John with a smile on his lips and turned to Mr. R. "Well, I was the one inviting you," Vince laughed, "and now that you've been close to the action, I need to know that I have the full support to continue doing what we're doing. In a moment, we will face the press and they'll bombard us with questions and speculations concerning the chances we took today and concerning Old Guy Tyler and his injury—which really is a major setback for us. They'll question how wise it was and what we'll do now. I need you to express unlimited faith and support in Bob Fisher and Hack Hampor. If anyone has an issue with that, please stay away from the press conference!"

Vince was very pleased, but not surprised, to see everyone coming to the press conference, looking proud and committed—just the way he wanted them to look.

****

The press lounge was packed with reporters and cameras. Vince worked his way through and mounted the podium.

"Gentlemen thanks for showing up today. Today we showed everyone who loves football what the game is all about. We ran into trouble, but managed to keep our heads cool and we were rewarded. I would like to thank Tyler for his presence on the sideline after his injury and to everyone in the whole organization for their support out there today."

The questions came as a regular bombardment as soon as Vince finished. The press wanted to know how the team would cope the next couple of weeks without Tyler, and they wanted to know how Vince would surprise his coming opponents.

Vince laughed at the last question. "Well, I would love to tell you but then I would have to kill you all, otherwise it wouldn't be a surprise, would it?" The whole room laughed, but nevertheless continued asking the same questions.

Towards the end of the conference, one of the older reporters got up and turned slightly towards the back of the room where John stood. As if he was asking both Vince and John, he said, "I have noticed an old friend of ours has been present almost any time we've seen you over the last couple of weeks. Would you care to share something about that with us?"

John was ready to answer, but Vince once again took the lead and in a slow but confident voice he said, "Well, most of you know Coach John and know what a well of experience he is. Although he's from a different sport, he knows a lot that can benefit any team and any coach in any sport. He has been kind enough to share some of his wisdom with me and the guys, and much of what you saw accomplished on the field today comes from the extras he has contributed. You all raised a very big question this summer about how ready I was to take over this team, and in some areas, I had to realize that some things are different than where I come from, but the game on the field is the same, so I've been brushing up on the things that aren't directly related to the tactics of the game. Coach John has been an important source of inspiration in that process. Thank you. Any further questions? If not, you all will excuse me. We have a celebration to enjoy."

"If you don't mind I would like to add a thing" the voice came from the corner and belonged to Herb Withers.

Most of the journalists were the same and they remembered last time Herb spoke and their attention quickly turned towards him, hoping that he again would provide headlines by attacking the coach, just as he had done only weeks ago.

"I can see a lot of familiar faces and most of you were here last time I spoke" he paused "I would like to make a statement!" again he paused and the room was filled with suspense "I would like to let you all know that I was wrong! I only saw things from my own perspective and I didn't look ahead at a brighter and better future for the team and the whole organization". Once again he paused and looked around creating eye contact with the people most of whom he knew so well.

"I really liked Coach Mac, that's no secret and he will always be a good friend of mine and a great coach and I was very skeptic about getting Coach Longman. Over the last two weeks Coach Longman has shown more bravery and guts than most men do in a lifetime. Not only has he turned a lot of things around in the team but he has at the same time had the humbleness to invite help and incorporate the wisdom of the organization and many others. Most head coaches that I have met have been stubborn soles and that's a good thing, they need to be, but with Coach Longman that stubbornness is combined with a heart and a brain!" Again a long pause and the room was so silent you could hear a pin fall onto the carpet.

"We still have a lot of hard work in front of us, but on behalf of myself and the other team captains, I would like to make it clear that we are behind him all the way and support his efforts of creating greatness! That's all, I have nothing more to add and as Coach said, we have a celebration to take care of!"

*****

Vince slowly chewed his toast. The early morning breakfast with John had become a natural thing, almost a ritual, and he was anxious to hear what reflections John had on the game and the way he had handled the press afterwards. Normally, Coach John beat him to the breakfast table. It was strange that he was not there when Vince arrived, and now, almost twenty minutes into the breakfast, John was still not there. Vince started to worry, got his cell phone out, and dialed the number. It didn't take long for John to pick up the phone.

"What took you so long?" Vince could hear John smiling through the phone and ignored the question.

Vince asked, "Where are you? I have been waiting for you since 7 a.m.!"

John walked through the door to the restaurant with a big grin on his face. As he sat down he started talking, "You know I was almost starving to death waiting for you to react. I've been sitting out in the foyer waiting to see how you would react. This morning's lesson was about the agreements we make and our accountability. We didn't have a specific agreement about meeting here at 7 a.m., but because we've done so every morning over the last two weeks or more, we've established a preceding behavior and based on that we could call that a kind of agreement. So when I don't show up, what are the consequences? How do we react to that, how much do we tolerate? Sometimes people break the rules or the agreements and we need to have some kind of reaction or consequence if you like to that."

Vince nodded as if he understood where John was going, but he didn't see the next thing coming.

"Yesterday before the press conference, you were very clear about everyone sticking to the pride and commitment and how everybody who attended should back you up or not be present. Compared to the first press conference I witnessed with you, you made a quantum leap. Everyone was there on time and ready and supportive of your moves. So far, so good. But you and I made an agreement when we embarked on this adventure together. We agreed that the official cover story for my presence was that I was writing a book and doing research, yet you revealed the whole thing without warning me. So what do you think happened on my way out of the clubhouse last night? Yeah right, I was held prisoner by the press for another hour!"

"I am so sorry. I didn't think that..." Vince would have said more but John interrupted him.

"No, you didn't think, but I know you had a very positive intention and I don't blame you. I just want to use it as an example of how fast and easy it is for people to forget their promises."

John looked at Vince and saw that he was truly sorry and struggling to find ways to apologize, but John just laughed. "Actually, I have to admit that despite the breach of our agreement, you really showed guts by doing just that! You made me proud and I'm not offended in the least. To admit that you are not perfect requires bravery especially in front of the press."

Vince sighed and smiled. "You almost had me on that one, and right you are. Although my intention was good, we had a different agreement and I didn't respect that. Point taken! Can I buy you dinner tonight?"

Both men laughed and debriefed the past day and its events. They extracted the learnings and when done, John looked at Vince. "I think you're ready to work your way through the rest of the season without me. There's still much to be done with the team, but I think that right now, the focus has to be on keeping what you have gained, keeping the momentum of the team, and making additional changes. Work should continue after the season is over and if you need me there, I'll be happy to drop by. What do you think, Mr. Longman?"

Vince slowly nodded. "I think you are right. I would love to have you here on my team for the rest of the season, but I also know that from here I need to do my job on my own and I feel ready to do so." As if he was sealing the adventure they had been on together, he continued, "Mr. Craft, it has been an honor. If there is anything I can do to repay you in any way, do not hesitate to call me, day or night." He extended his hand and the two men held each other's hand for a while with no further words exchanged. John got up and walked out without looking back.

*****

Now had this been a fairytale, the team would then have gone all the way and won the National Championship, but they didn't! They did, however, reach the finals and lost by only one point, making it the best season in the team's recent history. The praise of Vince Longman as the most successful young coach ever was the headline all over the nation and despite the loss, the whole organization felt proud of what they had accomplished.

*****

John had stayed busy since that morning he left Vince in the restaurant. Mr. R kept his word and put all his energy, network, and resources into the creation of John Craft Junior High Sports Academy, and by the end of the summer, he was proud to open it, standing next to Coach John when the opening ceremony took place. John chose to lead the school himself and was not only the school's Headmaster, but he also taught. He ran special classes for kids with really tough backgrounds and he committed to straighten them out. It was indeed one of these classes he was running this morning.

As usual, he was present in the room before class started, making himself available to each of the students. Nothing seemed out of the ordinary when he started the class, but very shortly afterwards, he heard from the speakers hanging above his door, "Headmaster Craft to the auditorium! Urgently!" He was baffled. What could it be? But no time for thinking, he apologized to the class, quickly gave them something to do and then left, almost running, worrying what might be.

He crashed through the doors to the auditorium, but much to his surprise, it was pitch dark in there and he thought to himself, "Did I just imagine the call over the speakers?"

"SURPRISE!"

The entire room roared as the lights came on. Every student in the school except the class he just left was in the auditorium. On the stage was Vince Longman, the whole assistant coaching team, and most of the football team.

Dumbbell Jack got up on the podium and looked at the crowd. "Kids, my name is Jack Keshigan, also known as Dumbbell Jack since I'm the physical coach on the team. Today I want to talk to you about change! I want to talk about what you can do if you accept that other people have skills and you open up to them and accept their gift of wisdom. Most of you probably know the story about how this school came about and how Coach John – or should I say Headmaster Craft? – how he came to the rescue of the football team in this city. Well, I for one was not so impressed with the idea. I've been working with John Craft since way back in my early years and I did my very best to get results. I was a stubborn young man mostly listening to myself and my own ideas and when change was needed I was not open to it. I rejected it and Coach John fired me, so you can probably imagine how I felt when he now was back and changes were needed. But Coach John doesn't do changes without a good reason, and he worked hard and diligently with each and every one of us and it made me realize how much he had to offer. I was slow in realizing it, but will never forget that he embraced me and accepted me, despite the past, so I'm here today, along with the whole team behind me, to embrace you and accept you, despite your pasts. You all have a great future and you deserve it, don't you?"

The room was quiet, but heads were nodding and Old Guy Tyler took over.

"I could tell you a similar story, but I want to talk to you about the whole idea of being a team. When you're a team, there is no 'I' in team, but to quote Michael Jordan, there is an 'I' in winning. So what I've learned is that the purpose of the team is to play together and to support and develop each other in order to generate that synergy and that the 'I' is about how much I can contribute to the team, not just to myself and my own good."

Many other contributed with short stories about the transformation of the team and each of them touched upon the little things that had made the big difference. Although different topics and stories, they all shared the same back bone: believe that you can, work hard to get there and things will happen. If you paid attention you could see that many from the team and the coaching staff had tears in their eyes, and you could also see the excitation and the appreciation in all the kids in the auditorium, who perhaps for the first time realized how fortunate they were to be at this brand new school, build on Coach John's idea of giving people a second chance.

It was an amazing scenario. Big football players talking about their past and their chances in life and how they had grabbed opportunity, but nothing was more impressive than when Vince got up as the very last person. For a moment he just stood there, saying nothing, just looking at the young people gathered. Then he looked over to Coach John.

"As so many of you know, I was hired as head coach before last season. It was a big opportunity for me. I was at first in doubt if I could make the jump to the pro level, but I was reassured that I could and that I would get all the help and the backing I would need, so I accepted and started working. The transition was far bigger than I could ever have imagined. The mechanics of a pro organization and the pro players are not the same as what I was used to. Money makes a big difference in people's behavior. If people don't have it, they sometimes do stupid behavior and I'm sure a lot of you know what I'm talking about. But what you may not know is that when they have a lot of it, they very often do even more stupid behavior. I learned this the hard way and, for sure, my results were not anywhere near my own or the team's expectations. Although it was still very early, I did start to question myself and blame myself for taking the job."

He paused for a moment. He had the full attention of everyone in the room, including his own staff and players. Several looked almost embarrassed, as if they knew only too well what kind of stupid behavior he was talking about. Vince didn't pay attention because his message was not intended for the players, but for the young men and women in front of him.

"One of the most stupid behaviors that took place last summer was my own. I thought I could handle the change by doing what I have always done. I kept doing the same thing, thinking I would get different results if I just kept doing it. But I'm here today to tell you that change doesn't come from continuing to do the same thing! Change comes from doing things differently!"

The room was now so quiet that you could hear a coin drop on the carpet. All of these young people had been accepted to this junior high based on their background and a sincere need to do things differently in order to get an education and a chance in life. They knew what Vince was talking about and they listened with every fiber in their soul.

"I was lucky! Someone believed in me and wanted me to succeed. Mr. Ridgeback, the owner of our franchise, called me and said he wanted to talk to me. I went there believing I would get fired, although still early in the season, but instead he told me that he had summoned someone who could work with me and he would try to convince this guy that he should come help me and the organization. This someone accepted the challenge and this is how I got to know one of the great men in this world, Coach John."

The suspense in the room was now at an all-time high, everybody waiting for each and every word from Vince. He paused, looked at John and then back to the audience.

"Coach John showed me the way. He didn't do the work for me. He taught me how and then I had to work hard to make it happen. We wanted change and we started doing things differently and, along with that, came the result. We made it happen because we believed it could happen. We sacrificed old habits knowing that we couldn't do what we had done before and get different outcomes…" He paused again for a while, took a deep breath in. "All of you here have been given that same chance to change and get results! My advice to you is grab it and believe in it. It will require hard work and sacrifices, but it is worth it, because the reward is not what you get, but what you can do."

He did say something more in the end, but it was drowned in applause and cheers from the audience. All the young men and women and the whole team and staff stood and cheered together, not so much for Vince, but more as an outburst of agreement with his message that things can happen if you believe in them, that if you work hard, results will come and that if you need change, you must be willing to do things differently!

****

The story could end here and it will, but it is worth noting that Vince Longman and his staff worked hard the entire off-season and kept focusing on where they could do things better and differently. The next season, they went undefeated and won the national championship, in itself a remarkable achievement. But even more remarkable were the results obtained by the athletes at John Craft Junior High Sports Academy, several of them taking national titles… Yes, even in the real world fairytales do exist!

Notes to yourself:

- ✓ *Things can happen if you believe in them.*

- ✓ *If you are committed and work hard, results will come. Luck happens more frequently to the well prepared!*

- ✓ *Don't expect change to happen by repeating the same behavior. If you need change, do things differently!*

ABOUT THE AUTHORS

Anders Piper, Denmark is the International Director of Sports Performance Coaching for the Society of Neuro-Linguistic Programming. He holds a Master of Science degree in Psychology and a he is also a Licensed Master Trainer of NLP with Society of NLP

Anders has an interesting background in sports. He has competed in both individual and team sports and he has been national champion 3 times and has competed at European level and knows the demands and the pressure that there can be on an athlete and the commitment it requires to be at the top level in your sport. You will benefit from his competitive nature and direct no-nonsense approach to training, coaching and success!

Today Anders work intensively with athletes and executives to help them improve their performance and he is also the Program Director for the Internationally recognized certification training "Licensed Sports Performance Coach". You can read more about Anders and the training programs on:

www.inlpsa.com

Alessandro Mora is a Licensed Master Trainer of Neuro-Linguistic programming and Peak Performance Coach. He has extensive experience as peak performance coach in both individual and team sports. Amongst the sports he has coached are volleyball, football, basketball, rugby, tennis, golf, archery, dance, swimming, diving, running, cycling, horse riding, race car driving, and many others.

He coaches international athletes and teams in order to improve their performance and results. Alessandro teaches NLP, coaching, team building and communication skills applied to sport and business all over Italy, where he co-created the unique 'Ekis Master in Coaching', one of the most exclusive programs where you can learn how to become a Pro Peak Performance Coach.

You can read more about Alessandro and the training programs on:

www.pnlekis.com

20519068R00116

Made in the USA
Charleston, SC
16 July 2013